THE SKIN OF CULTURE

DERRICK DE KERCKHOVE

THE SKIN OF CULTURE

INVESTIGATING THE NEW ELECTRONIC REALITY

EDITED BY

CHRISTOPHER DEWDNEY

A Patrick Crean Book

SOMERVILLE HOUSE PUBLISHING

TORONTO

Canadian Cataloguing in Publication Data

De Kerckhove, Derrick
The skin of culture : investigating the new
electronic reality : from the work
of Derrick de Kerckhove

ISBN 1-895897-45-9

1. Mass media – Social aspects. 2. Technology –
Social aspects. I. Dewdney, Christopher, 1951-
II. Title

P90.D45   302.23'4   C95-930736-2

Design: Gordon Robertson
Copyeditor: Ruth Chernia
Printed in Canada

A Patrick Crean Book

Published by Somerville House Publishing,
a division of Somerville House Books Limited,
3080 Yonge Street, Suite 5000, Toronto, Ontario M4N 3N1

Somerville House Publishing acknowledges the financial assis-
tance of the Ontario Publishing Centre, the Ontario
Arts Council, the Ontario Development Corporation,
and the Department of Communications.

"In the electric age, we wear all mankind as our skin."

– Marshall McLuhan

CONTENTS

INTRODUCTION

S OME YEARS AGO *The Times Literary Supplement* claimed that the Toronto of Harold Innis, Eric Havelock and Marshall McLuhan was "for a brief period the intellectual centre of the world."[1] The article went on to say that in Toronto "a new theory was born, the theory of the primacy of communication in the structuring of human cultures and the human mind."

The period that the article referred to, the late fifties and sixties, was indeed a seminal decade in communications theory. But it was Marshall McLuhan, more than Innis or Havelock, who caught the public's imagination. With his self-avowed "Catholic paranoia," McLuhan had hit upon a technique of media analysis that had tremendous consequences. The publication of *The Gutenberg Galaxy* in 1962 astonished readers around the world. In one stroke, McLuhan had set the scholastic community on its ear and captured the attention of the media. Never had such an enigmatic seer aroused people's curiosity in such a powerful way. Today, his phrases and aphorisms are standard terms in our contemporary vocabulary.

Since Marshall McLuhan's death, in 1980, there has been much speculation about his true heir. McLuhan spawned dozens of self-proclaimed gurus from Alvin Toffler to Faith Popcorn, while in universities across North America and Europe, media studies departments gave rise to more contenders with the weight of academe behind them. By tracing an unbroken lineage, however, the most probable inheritor of McLuhan's mantle is McLuhan's own colleague, the irreverent and erudite Derrick de Kerckhove.

Best known as the director of the McLuhan Program in Culture and Technology at the University of Toronto, Derrick de Kerckhove has been contributing to the on-going debate about the ultimate effects of communications and media technology for over two decades. His close association with Marshall McLuhan during the seventies, as translator, assistant and co-author, gave him privileged access to the inner workings of the mind of this century's pre-eminent media philosopher. Now, as McLuhan's successor at the head of the world's foremost institute of media studies, the McLuhan Program in Culture and Technology, de Kerckhove is positioned to continue the work of Marshall McLuhan.

In the years since McLuhan's death, de Kerckhove has been active on several fronts. He was at the centre of an international network of scholars, artists and communications analysts dedicated to the study of McLuhan's vision of the electronic media. This was an invaluable proving ground for his own theories, enabling him to test his ideas with many experts. Meanwhile he has maintained a full course load as a professor in the French Department at the University of Toronto, and because of his association with the University he was able to establish the McLuhan Program in Culture and Technology, which is presently situated in McLuhan's famous coach house on the university's campus. Throughout this time, he has worked as a media consultant for telecommunications firms, various levels of government, businesses and television networks.

To watch Derrick de Kerckhove in operation at the Program in Culture and Technology is to witness both his intensity and his multi-track capability. On a typical afternoon he negotiates a chaotic swirl of meetings with media theorists, virtual reality artists, students, businessmen, scientists and scholars. One moment he will be demonstrating the Program's latest technological gadget and a few seconds later he will be on the phone to a colleague in Europe. In the background the fax machine chatters incessantly. His mind is clearly lateral and his conversation brims with anecdotes, tangents and nuggets of data. By necessity, de Kerckhove is an inveterate traveller and for him the global village is a physical reality. He virtually lives on jets, often airborne on his way to Europe, the United States or Japan. Also, he is directly acquainted with the various media he describes in *The Skin of Culture* because they are pragmatic parts of his workaday reality. He has been videoconferencing for almost a decade, and for more than a decade he has been immersing himself in virtual reality at various stages of its development. With his practical knowledge of the on-going computer and telecommunications revolution, and his playful, speculative mind, de Kerckhove is well situated to consider our new reality.

In this book, his first major Canadian publication, Derrick de Kerckhove demonstrates why he is Canada's media prophet laureate. By building on McLuhan's work, de Kerckhove has extended and deepened some of McLuhan's insights, as well as developing his own original and provocative theories. *The Skin of Culture* is an overview of his research and speculations culled from the last decade. In it, the breadth and profundity of his vision is laid out for first time. The culmination of years of research and consultation, *The Skin of Culture* looks at how the electronic media have extended not only our nervous systems and bodies, but also our psychology.

Television, for instance, de Kerckhove describes as a collective organ of teledemocracy that uses market surveys and polls to scan the social body like an X-ray. He maintains that this is because television is a projection of our emotional unconscious, and that for this reason and because it is a "mass medium," television is a collective externalization of its audience's psychology. He goes on to say that television, as a result of this inverted psychology, has parachuted a new political system in our laps in a fait accompli, but that we haven't fully realized how profoundly it has already changed our social agenda. He describes this new political reality as a functional, participatory democracy, *telecracy*, that may well play directly into the hands of populists. Looking beyond these effects, he claims that computers are about to "swallow" television and that the forthcoming populist revolution will itself eventually succumb along with broadcast television.

Also provocative, though supported by behavioural science, are his theories about the physical effects of television on both our bodies and our nervous systems, particularly as these are combined in our neuromuscular systems. He argues that television demonstrably talks to the body but not the mind, and that we continuously re-enact what we see on television, almost instantaneously, with sub-muscularized responses. Television violence, he says, physically hits us—a preposterous claim were it not for the persuasive laboratory experiments that led him to this conclusion.

Expanding on his established reputation as a literacy and language theorist, de Kerckhove explains in two essays the historical effect that the technologies of language and writing have had on humans. He claims that these linguistic precedents frame our present media revolutions in both a technological and biological sense, and that language and alphabets constitute a kind of "software" that predisposed us to our technologies. Proposing a symbiotic relation between intelligence and language, de Kerckhove goes on to explain how writing amplifies intelligence.

One of the more fascinating sidelights in de Kerckhove's linguistic musings are his revelations about the origin and function of money. He traces the evolution of money from its twin birth with writing in Sumeria to its present, electric incarnation as a wave of electromagnetic pulses skimming around the world at the speed of light. He likens the flow of money around the globe to the ticking of the CPU timer in a computer that co-ordinates all its processing functions. In his vision, money is transformed into a purely symbolic, informational valve of social exchange. He also contends that inflationary periods are the invariable response of monetary markets to technological change. As money becomes lighter and lighter, more and more electronic he says, it will offer less and less resistance to transactions. In a massless state, currencies will become a sort of electric current themselves, fuelling the operations of a techno-cultural engine, a collective machine whose complexity we can only guess at.

Also included is de Kerckhove's disturbing analysis of the far from unifying effects that globalization will have on social structures. He suggests that war and nationalism may be on the rise as a result. *The Skin of Culture* warns that our planet is at a precarious turning point that can lead either to fragmentation or further globalization, and that only by designing our technologies, instead of letting them design us, will we be able to avert social catastrophe. As Marshall McLuhan did before him, he also contends that what appear to be marginal qualities of the media often have the most powerful effects. Understanding and controlling these qualities may turn out to be one of the most crucial undertakings of our species, for new technologies wage war upon the culture they emerge into.

The political ramifications of the new media appear to be equally momentous. The fall of the Berlin Wall and the end of the Cold War were, according to de Kerckhove, inevitable events brought about by electronic telecommunications and information processing systems, as well as by television. He then turns his attention to the West and the rise of multinationals in the era of tertiary capitalism, illustrating how multinationals are already redefining borders and national identities. Not only does he see trade blocs as the new national boundaries, he also claims that the culture of business is becoming global culture itself. He sees political correctness as a symptom of sensitization, a direct result of the therapeutic realm of telecracy, and he cautions that we are not out of the woods yet, for our biological reality is about to reassert itself. He speculates that gender specializations of the brain and senses may influence the political reality of the cyber-electric environment. After demonstrating how electronic media are faster than democratic causality, he introduces a convincing argument that verifies what we all intuitively suspect—that polls are subtle manipulations. Surprisingly, however, it appears that they are manipulated collectively. This is the first technological explanation of Chomsky's theory of "the manufacture of consent."

De Kerckhove's predictions of how the looming technological revolution will touch us personally are detailed and fascinating. Our machines will be customized to talk to us, recognize us, anticipate us. Not only that, we will wear some of them! Our home entertainment systems will be designed around how they feel rather than how they look. Virtual reality, as well as voice-activated, ultra-fast home processors, will enact our desires so quickly that in the long run, changing our personal identity will become a primary entertainment, like a cosmetic surgery of the psyche. In the telecomputer networks of the future, individuals will become producers as much as consumers because as broadcast systems break down into smaller and smaller units, the creative impetus of individuals will change them from consumers to Toffler's "prosumers."

In de Kerckhove's analysis of Japanese culture, the metaphors thrown-off by Godzilla and Transformers (shape-shifting toys developed in Japan that are half human, half machine) find concrete applications. He explains how Japanese cultural values are in harmony with electronic cultural influences and why the Japanese have adapted so quickly to the new technologies. He then borrows a key concept from Japanese culture to illustrate how we can fast-forward our own understanding of the new cybernetic realm.

The Skin of Culture contains serious predictions that businesses, administrators and anyone else involved in the increasingly complex world of media and telecommunications can hardly afford to ignore. When McLuhan predicted the end of *Life* magazine because it was too print oriented, and this at the height of its circulation, no one would have guessed his prophecy would come true within a decade. By contrast, the assertions that de Kerckhove makes are, if anything, cautious, achieved by years of research and consideration, even if at first glance they may appear audacious. At the very least *The Skin of Culture* represents a realistic look at five or ten years down the pike, and a five-to-ten-year edge in the fast-moving business of telecommunications can make a huge difference. Trend watchers of all persuasions will have a surfeit of scenarios to choose from, for *The Skin of Culture* provides a smorgasbord of emerging patterns.

Where Derrick de Kerckhove most resembles Marshall McLuhan is in his emphasis on orality and tactility, particularly as they relate to language and the way we process our sensory reality. He proposes that, although the electronic media are reversing the effects of literacy and language, this is not necessarily a bad thing, because we are returning to oral culture from our predominately literate one. He speculates that in the forthcoming oral-cybernetic culture of information ignorance will become a valuable commodity because 'unprogrammed' individuals will have a functional edge over 'programmed' ones. The flexibility of the ignorant will arise from the fact that they will not have to fight old biases and mind sets to learn new technologies.

Enigmatically, he suggests that virtual reality is relentless and has its own agenda, a teleological supposition that is reminiscent of Terrence McKenna, the American ethnobotanist who writes about hallucinogenic realities. De Kerckhove believes that virtual reality, with simulated tactility, is about to revolutionize our most neglected media sense—touch, and turn it into a cognitive extension of our minds; that inner space, quantum physics and nanotechnology, is opening up a new frontier as capacious as outer space; that as technology and communications speed up we will be able to slow down and discover true tranquillity. This tranquillity may set the stage for a necessary psychological transformation, because ultimately, cybertechnical power will confer with it the obligation for self-knowledge.

De Kerckhove's most compelling forecasts, however, concern our great, collective undertakings as a species. We are about to create a collective mind he says, one that will exceed the capabilities of any individual human. This will happen because of emergent properties, which are those properties that can suddenly arise when any dynamic, interconnected system gets to a certain point of complexity. A complex system can behave in a manner similar to a living organism and in ways totally unanticipated by the engineers who built it. The groundwork for the collective mind will be laid by a political globalization whose initial stages will be accomplished invisibly by the convergence of television, telephones and computers. Internet is the nascent fetus of this collective brain, and smaller components of the final global consciousness are already forming within the interconections of cable networks, telecommunications systems and data banks, not to mention the cybernetic think tanks soon to link researchers in commutative brains that will truly be the sum of their parts. As de Kerckhove points out, Europe is well on the way to unifying into a collective, telecommunicative information-processing entity.

One of the things that distinguishes de Kerckhove's theories is the ease with which he incorporates the findings of other disciplines into his philosphy. He gleans data from fields as diverse as neurobiology, behaviourism, broadcast television, business, linguistics and art, as well as from the observations of other media thinkers. This bricolage is a characteristic of his deeply held conviction that, increasingly, our most original and important discoveries will be made in the realm of interdisciplinary studies. And yet the synthesis that Derrick de Kerckhove achieves in this work still exceeds the synergy of its origins. His originality is unparalleled.

– Christopher Dewdney

CHAPTER ONE

TECHNO-PSYCHOLOGY

THE EFFECTS OF ELECTRIC TECHNOLOGIES

T HE VERY FIRST TIME I saw a fax machine was early in 1972, at the University of Toronto's Centre for Culture and Technology, then directed by Marshall McLuhan. McLuhan had wanted me to see the new contraption and to be on hand for translations. He was expecting a message from the French Minister of Cultural Affairs—the celebrated novelist André Malraux—and, of course, he planned to send a message back in French. The idea, I think, was to test the system transatlantically. Malraux himself didn't turn up, but one of his assistants did send a message of greetings from the Minister and we sent one back. I remember feeling no disappointment at Malraux's no-show, because my attention was completely overwhelmed by this extraordinary machine. It seemed to kiss the telephone and whisper a written message in its ear.

TECH-LAG

The same machine was used a few years later by Salvador Dali. He sent a drawing from New York in apology for not being able to attend a major conference on Celtic Consciousness, to which he had been invited as one of the keynote speakers. Seeing Dali's fax and reflecting on the status of the famous painter's signature, I envied those lucky enough to be able to afford such technology. To my surprise, years went by without anybody talking about fax machines, not even around McLuhan. The closest thing to a fax machine I saw in ten years was an old Texas Instruments Teletype, which a friend lent me for a few days in 1982.

By 1985 though, if you didn't have a fax machine or access to a fax machine, you were obviously completely out of touch with reality. What had happened? Why did it take so long for people to realize that they simply couldn't live without fax machines? A similar delay postponed telephone answering systems that were available and even aggressively marketed in the mid-sixties. They only took off in the late seventies. The same thing has happened with no less a technology than television that, after being used sporadically as early as 1928, only really came out of mothballs after the Second World War. An identical delay is currently postponing videoconferencing, which must eventually explode on to the market just like the fax machine did.[2]

Of course, there's always a technical or bottom-line explanation for everything. What happened with the fax machine techno-lag is that, in the early seventies, international telephone systems were not ready to take on another load. Meanwhile, the Japanese, who had a vested interest in finding ways to communicate their unwieldy writing system, had stepped up research and development to improve fax technology. They reduced its demands on the carrier and brought down the price. But that's only half the story. The other half is that the best and most useful technology in the world cannot impose itself on an unprepared public. And the reason is that there may be no room for it in our collective psychology. At least, not yet.

TECHNO-FETISHISM

On the other hand, when consumer technologies finally are introduced into our lives, they can generate a kind of fetishistic obsession in their users, something McLuhan once dubbed the "narcosis of Narcissus." Indeed, we seem to want our personal machines, whether it is a car or a computer, to be endowed with powers far in excess of the use we may make of them. Though few of us would seriously consider automobile racing, let alone have the chance to practise it, we want our Toyota to be capable of being driven at twice the expressway speed limit. The amateur photographer might not consider carrying all his groceries home from the store, but he'll be willingly weighed down with equipment, even during a mountain climb, rather than be found without the latest product from Nikon or Minolta. From the moment they take to computers, our children develop a kind of speed addiction that makes them howl and kick if their favourite programs take more than a nanosecond to come on-line.

Where other cultural observers might have cited forces of marketing, McLuhan saw in this phenomenon a purely psychological pattern of narcissistic identification with the power of our toys. I see it as the proof that we are indeed becoming cyborgs, and that, as each technology extends one of our faculties and transcends our physical limitations, we are inspired to acquire the very best extension of our own body. When we buy our home video system, we want it to perform every possible editing function, not because we will ever use them, but because we would feel handicapped and inadequate without them.

This is probably a healthy approach, not a pathology. Indeed, it suggests that we are perfectly capable of integrating devices into our identity, certainly into our bodies. Such an ability prepares the ground for the necessary development of a new psychology, one better equipped to deal with the world ahead. Presently, we react too cautiously and slowly. Some of us are about to carry the psychological make-up of nineteenth-century country bumpkins into the twenty-first century. Our political and educational systems are trailing far behind our technology and our marketing, themselves patterned according to criteria good enough to operate commercial enterprises, but hardly adequate to deal with the world's changing problems and values.

TECHNO-PSYCHOLOGY

It's a truism to say we don't miss what we don't know and another to say that advertising creates needs that aren't there in the first place. Such banalities are based on the unquestioned assumption that all men and women were created not only equal, but once and for all and forever the same. Nothing could be further from the facts of life. We are forever being made and remade by our own inventions. The myth of humanity's base-line universality is just a product of an eighteenth-century philosopher's wishful thinking.

Our psychological reality is not a "natural" thing. It is partially dependent upon the way our environment, including our own technological extensions, affects us. One way to understand psychology, both as a fact of life and as a science, is to propose that its purpose is to provide a comprehensive and self-updating interpretation of our lives as they are being affected by our ever-changing cultural ground. Hence, among its many regulating functions, psychology's role may be to interpret and to integrate the effects of technology upon us. One of the functions of our personal psychology is to create an illusion of continuity when there are major cultural and technological breaks and, thus, to slow down the effects of technological feedback on our nervous system. If we did not have some sort of personal stabilizing environment, we would be in a permanent state of shell shock from dealing with the cultural trauma of new technologies. We would be like Chancy Gardiner, the main character in Jerzy Kosinski's novel *Being There*. After living his whole adult life in front of television, Chancy walks out into the street for the first time and finds to his utter dismay that, for some unaccountable reason, his remote control no longer works.

"Techno-psychology" is the study of the psychological condition of people under the influence of technological innovation. Techno-psychology may be all the more relevant now that there are technological extensions to our psychological faculties. Techno-psychology could be proposed for the attention of investigators of culture and psychology as the field of activities of psychotechnologies.

PSYCHOTECHNOLOGIES

I have coined the term "psychotechology," patterned on the model of biotechnology, to define any technology that emulates, extends or amplifies the powers of our minds. For example, while television is generally perceived only as a one-way conduit for audio-visual material, it might be helpful to psychologists to see it as an extension of our eyes and ears into the places where the images originate. When you understand television in this way, it matters little whether programming is live or recorded. Indeed, telephone, radio, television, computers and other media combine to create environments that, together, establish intermediate realms of information-processing. These are the realms of psychotechnologies. Seen from this vantage, television becomes our collective imagination projected outside our bodies, combining in a consensual, electronic teledemocracy. TV is literally, as Bill Moyers called it, a "public mind."[3]

This public realm is most explicit during videoconferencing. With videoconferencing and videophones, television approaches the flexibility and instantaneous communication afforded by the telephone. Indeed, such technologies not only extend the sending and receiving properties of consciousness, they also penetrate and modify the consciousness of their users. Virtual reality is closer still. It adds touch to sight and sound and is as near to 'mainlining' the human nervous system as any technology has ever been. With virtual reality and telepresence robotics we literally project our consciousness outside our bodies and see it 'objectively.' This is the first time that humans have been able to do this.

With television and computers we have moved information processing from within our brains to screens in front of, rather than behind, our eyes. Video technologies relate not only to our brain, but to our whole nervous system and our senses, creating conditions for a new psychology. We have yet to come to terms with our relationship to our screens. It may help to understand that TV does not compete with books, but suggests something entirely different. It proposes a collective imagination as something we can actually consume,

although not yet directly participate in. That essential feature, interaction, a capability that guarantees our individual autonomy within
the powerful trend of psychotechnological collectivization, is provided by computers and even more so by computer networks.

CHAPTER TWO

TELEVISION

THE COLLECTIVE IMAGINATION

THE NEW MEDIA CONTEXT

S TEVEN KLINE is the Director of the Media Analysis Lab at Simon Fraser University in Vancouver. He and his brother Rob have invented a sophisticated system to analyze people's physiological responses to anything they are being shown. Anything, everything and, especially, television. Kline's work on the impact of television advertising and programming is well-known. Recently, Stephen and his brother invited me to be one of their guinea pigs. They wired me to a computer with various skin-response devices. They attached one to my left middle finger for skin conductivity, another to my forehead—presumably to probe my brain activity—a third to my left wrist to take my pulse and the last over my heart area to monitor circulation. Another device, a rather crude joystick, was placed in my right hand. By pushing it forwards or backwards, I could indicate whether I liked or disliked what I was watching. Then Rob and Stephen left the lab and the show began.

I watched a fast paced jumble of typical viewing fare: sex, advertising, news, talk shows, sentimentality and tedium. The cuts seemed to average around fifteen seconds each. By normal TV standards, that speed does not appear to be excessive, though in my new role as a knee-jerk critic, I found it very difficult to keep up the pace with the joystick. By the end of the twenty-minute experiment, I was thoroughly frustrated, having failed to express much more than limp-wristed approvals or disapprovals. For many cuts, I hadn't had enough time to express anything at all.

When Rob and Stephen came back to rewind the tape and check the graphs on the computer, I told them my feeling of helplessness. They laughed and invited me to watch the screen while they replayed the tape in sync with the data. To my absolute amazement, I saw that every cut, every jolt, every change of image had been recorded by one sensor or another and fed into the computer. I could see the busy outlines of the graphs corresponding to my skin conductivity, pulse, heartbeat and to whatever mysterious response my forehead had been giving. I was flabbergasted. As I was labouring to express an opinion, my whole body had been listening and watching and reacting instantaneously.

TV TALKS TO THE BODY, NOT THE MIND

I drew two important conclusions from that experience. The first is that television talks primarily to the body, not to the mind. This is something I'd suspected for several years. The second conclusion was that, if the video screen has such a direct impact on my nervous system and my emotions, and so little effect on my mind, then most of the information-processing was actually being performed by the screen. These are hypotheses I want to explore in this study of our ubiquitous, intimate and yet so little-known relationships to our screens: our videominds.

FELT-MEANING

Woody Allen says to Diane Keaton, while driving in a taxi in *Manhattan:* "You're so beautiful, I can hardly keep my eyes on the meter."

Why is it so difficult, if not impossible, to concentrate when the TV is on? Because television is hypnotically involving: any movement on the screen attracts our attention as automatically as if someone had just touched us. Our eyes are dragged towards the screen like iron to a magnet.

ORIENTING AND DEFENSIVE RESPONSES

Understanding our television culture depends upon understanding how and why television fascinates us beyond our conscious control As I've proved to myself with the Kline brothers' experiment, my neuromuscular system constantly follows images on video, even if my mind occasionally wanders. This is involuntary because of our antediluvian biological programming: the autonomic nervous systems of higher mammals are trained to respond to any perceptible change in the environment that might be relevant to survival. We are conditioned to respond involuntarily to any kind of stimulation, internal or external, with what in clinical psychophysiology is called the Orienting Response (OR). This will either draw our attention towards the stimulus or alert the Defensive Response, which makes us recoil from it.

Now, you may well ask, in what way is TV relevant to our survival? In terms of content, not much. But television's principal action, as McLuhan never tired of repeating, happens not at the level of content but at the level of the medium itself, with the flickering light of the electron beam scanner. The changes and cuts in the shows provoke continuous OR's, drawing attention without necessarily satisfying it. In life, we accommodate stimuli as we get to know them: either we recognize them immediately or we quickly develop a strategy to deal with them. A completed response to a stimulus is called a closure. So in life, most stimuli awake an OR, call for a closure and receive it. With television, though, we are never done with the initial stimulus: TV provokes rapid successions of OR's without allowing time for closure.

THE "COLLAPSE OF THE INTERVAL" BETWEEN STIMULUS AND RESPONSE

In a paper on cognitive responses to television, German media theorist Hertha Sturm made an important observation. When we watch television, we are denied enough time to integrate the information on a fully conscious basis.

> Rapidly changing presentations impair verbalization. Among these are uninterpreted changes in viewing angle, unpredictable flip-flops from picture to text or from text to picture. When confronted with rapidly changing presentations and speeded-up action, the viewer is literally driven from image to image. This demands constantly new and unexpected adaptation to perceptual stimulation. As a result the viewer is no longer able to keep up and ceases to internally label. When this occurs, we found, the individual acts and reacts with heightened physiological arousal which in turn results in a reduction of comprehension. The viewer becomes, so to speak, a victim of an external force, of rapid audio-visual sequencing.[4]

Picking up on this theme, Edward Renouf Slopek, a McGill University communications researcher and McLuhan Program Associate, coined the expression "collapsing the interval" to indicate that TV eliminates the distancing effect—the interval between stimulus and response—and the time to process the information in our conscious mind.[5] The suggestion is that television leaves us little if any time to reflect on what we are watching.

JOLTS-PER-MINUTE (JPM'S) AND THE "MISSING HALF-SECOND"

Orienting responses elicited by television are quite different from those elicited by the cinema. The light from the video screen does not bounce back into our eyes, it comes right at us through the screen, challenging us to respond, like the spotlight of the police interrogator in a movie. Hertha Sturm claims that it takes the mind at least half a second to provide proper closure to complex stimuli. She claims that TV denies this to the viewer, in what she terms "the missing half-second syndrome." It certainly took my mind several seconds to deal, albeit inadequately, with the material compiled by Stephen Kline. Sturm is probably correct in implying that television programming is deliberately geared to preventing verbalized responses, so as to make us easy victims of advertising messages.

Recently, Toronto media critic Morris Wolfe created the concept of "jolts-per-minute"—or JPM's—to describe how TV shows hit us.[6] The notion behind JPM's is that it takes a critical number of cuts to prevent the viewer from falling asleep or switching channels. TV must zap the zapper before he or she zaps the channel. JPM's that keep the attention alive may also prevent cognitive closure.

SUB-MUSCULARIZATION AND "FELT MEANING"

However much people moralize, this is not necessarily a bad thing. One effect of the collapse of the interval is that in order to make sense of the rapid images we must somehow emulate the action with our bodies. Just as children faced with a new concept often find it helpful to act it out, we follow TV action with our bodies and even imitate the odd expression to better interpret it. This is what I call the "sub-muscularization effect"—analogous to the "sub-vocalization" strategy adopted by slow readers. Sub-muscularization is the interpretation of motion and action by a sort of sensorimotor mimicry involving the whole body. I suggest that we interpret gestures, postures and expressions on TV with a kind of sub-muscular response, expressed in muscle tone and stress factors.* Thus, 'television sense' is not the same as 'book sense.' It is closer to what the American psychologist and philosopher, Eugene T. Gendlin, call "felt meaning."

Gendlin defines felt-meaning as "the equivalent of hundreds of thousands of cognitive operations" done in a split second by the body in response to stimuli.7 Felt-meaning could be said to be a product of sub-muscularization. Indeed, as we experience events in our immediate surroundings, we store their relevant effects in various ways within our neuromuscular system. That is precisely what Hans Selye called stress. The Montreal-based clinical psychologist developed the theory of General Adaptive Syndrome (GAS) to account for the way we absorb the pressures of daily life, and how our body helps us to manage stress by sorting and storing stress's energy.

Although we know that we stop breathing when we are anxious or that we blush when we are put to shame, we are not usually aware of physical events happening within our bodies when we respond to people and situations. Felt-meaning is rarely conscious. But, in the background, it regulates and conditions our overall response to everyday matters. Felt-meaning precedes logic and may be more comprehensive than thought. Thus, the deeper effect of television might occur at the level of felt-meaning, offering little chance of response. Television evokes Orienting Responses that are woven into the fabric of our neuromuscular system.

"GRAZING AND ZAPPING IS THE WAY WE ATTEND TO EVERYTHING"

With this comment, social critic Michael Ignatieff condemned television. It probably reflects the opinion of many Canadians when he

---

* The need for this kind of patterning can be observed in people's behaviour on the telephone where we usually accompany our sentences with many gestures and movements that we use in face-to-face conversation; perhaps this is because such physical involvement helps us to make sense of what we are saying.

claims that "TV is turning us into a clever but shallow culture." It is easy to heap blame upon television. Often, without more than a hunch to go on, people attribute to television the instigation of social evils, everything from rape and murder to cynical apathy. Recently, a group of committed citizens in Vancouver felt so strongly about the dangers of television that they commissioned a series of TV ads to discourage people from watching. ("This sight is bad for you: stop looking right now.")

There are arguments about programming, ethics, aesthetics and invasions of privacy. But only a handful of critics, people like Jerry Mander, George Gerbner, Joshua Meyrowitz, Neil Postman and, certainly, McLuhan, have begun to understand the deeper message of the medium. TV is challenging our previously dominant, literate mindset by substituting its own tactile, collective orality. It threatens the sacrosanct autonomy we have acquired through reading and writing.

YOU DON'T WATCH TV, TV WATCHES YOU

There is not much that is "innocent" about the way we use our eyes. The following observation is by Jean-Marie Pradier, a professor of drama at the University of Paris and founder of an international association on Organized Human Performing Behaviours (OHPB).

> Social life, sexuality, and aggression are mainly ruled by visual components. This is perhaps why gazing is so severely controlled by precise codes and display rules. It is also why most of the human cultures have created freely viewed objects (paintings, sculptures, photographs, films) and freely viewed individuals (sportsmen and women, dancers, actors, and actresses, but also prostitutes, priests and public figures) along with free viewing spaces and events (theatre, carnival, hot urban districts) where it is possible to be a voyeur.[8]

Is television a free-viewing area? The relevance of this question was brought home to me at a clever video art installation by Mit Mitropoulos, a Greek communication artist from MIT. In *Face to Face*, two live participants sit back to back and converse with each other's images in real time on closed-circuit TV. Deceptively simple, the experience was unforgettable when I participated as one of the conversational partners. Irrespective of whether I did or didn't know my partner beforehand, I felt as if there were none of the usual barriers to staring someone right in the face. You could almost pick your nose in the context of this new electronic intimacy. True, I measured for the first time the extent to which we are terrified of faces in live contact, but what struck me more was that for the last thirty years we have unwittingly been watching our TV personalities without a trace of shyness. TV voyeurism is the "uncensored gaze." Perhaps television does provide a free-viewing area.

Or so it seems. The deep involvement required by viewing and the fact that most of our responses are involuntary bear witness to the changing power relationship between consumer and producer. When we read, we scan the books, we are in control. But when we watch TV, it is the TV scanner that 'reads' us. Our retinas are the direct object of the electron beam. When scanning meets glancing, and makes eye contact between man and machine, the machine's glance is the more powerful. In front of the television set, our defences are down; we are vulnerable and susceptible to multi-sensory seduction. Thus, the real meaning of Prime Time could be "priming time," that is, the best time to prime the mind of the television viewer. As Tony Schwartz, New York advertising executive and TV critic, suggested, "TV is not a window on the world, it's a window on the consumer."9

"GLANCING" VERSUS "SCANNING"

RCA's Herbert Krugman made headlines in the early seventies with his hypothesis that television talked to the right brain while books addressed the left—the more rational part of our grey matter. He suggested that TV puts the left brain to sleep. This may be true, but no amount of investigation has proven it to anyone's satisfaction. In fact, there is no need to invoke controversial brain localization here. The simple explanation that TV talks to the body rather than the mind says much more about television overriding our critical faculties.

However, Krugman later made a much more interesting suggestion that nobody picked up. He proposed that children brought up in front of television would not look at things the way kids normally do. Instead of using their eyes sequentially, as if they had been trained by print, Krugman suggested that they would take "quick looks."

> Television teaches the young child to "learn to learn" in a very special manner, to some extent before he can talk and, in many low socioeconomic status (SES) families or semiliterate societies, before he has ever looked at a book. So the child learns to learn by quick looks. Later, if the child is in a society where reading is required, he confronts the new "learn to learn" medium with the habit he has picked up earlier from TV. He tries to comprehend print via quick looks. It doesn't work. Learning to read is difficult, hard—and this comes as a surprise, an intolerable one in many cases.[10]

If this hypothesis is true, then our information-processing strategies have changed radically with the advent of TV.

When some young children are observed reading, it appears that they do not scan the text with the type of saccadic eye movements characteristic of the trained reader, but "throw their eyes" on the page as if they were transferring their visual strategy from the TV screen to the text. They seem to glance at things, looking at them several times as if they were compiling a picture to make sense of the page. This may have an important cognitive impact: Instead of scanning text to create and store images, children who watch TV must quickly generalize from loosely connected fragments and reconstitute the object of vision. This is very different from labelling objects and stringing them together in coherent sentences.

Text requires elaborate rules and conventions to avoid ambiguity. No wonder we need training to learn to read, and further education to interpret text fully. Nobody needs any instruction to watch TV. With TV, we are constantly rebuilding images that are neither complete on the screen nor in our mind. This is a dynamic process that bears some of the characteristics of our nervous systems. TV cuts up information into minimal and often unconnected segments, jamming together as much as possible in the shortest possible time. We complete the picture, making instant generalizations from a few clues. At the same time, programmers and editors have learned to take advantage of our readiness to fill in the gaps. This doesn't imply that we are making sense, just that we are making images. Making sense is another thing altogether, which doesn't seem to be essential for watching TV.

EDITING VERSUS MODULATING

Television, following the ways of film, adopted cinematographic editing as the norm. But since its medium is the electromagnetic pulse, TV is closer to music than to photography. As a completely electronic device, like the telephone or the radio, television is a modulator. To edit a film or an image, we have to cut it and piece it together with other cuts. We edit images to a storyline in our minds, adjusting them to fit the text. Film editing is a similar process, except that it is done outside our mind. In a manner of speaking, when we watch a film it is our own mind that is being edited on the spot.

With television the rapid manipulation of our neurophysiological responses, our felt-meaning system, goes well beyond frame-by-frame editing. It is so rapid, so continuous and so forceful that it's more like a magnetic modulation of our sensibility. Television modulates our emotions and our imaginations in a way comparable to the power of music. That is why the rock video is a natural television creature.

This is another aspect of the mysteriously tactile dimension that McLuhan attributed to television. When he suggested in later books that "the medium is the massage," making fun of his own celebrated aphorism, what he meant was that television caresses us and rubs its meaning under our skin.

TV prefers repetition to analysis and myths to facts. It brands its icons on our psyche as well as on the walls of our cities. Homogenization spreads like wildfire via TV, as nobody wants to be caught out of style. Any shopping mall is 'walk-on' TV. TV sounds, colours and shapes are the sensory expressions of our collective sensibility.[11] But TV regimentation of our sensibility takes other forms too, like canned laughter and applause or, a more subtle lever, electronic polling. Most of what appears in news bulletins and documentaries is pre-digested and presented in stereotyped format for a quick bite, like fast-food. Hasn't TV created a mass culture, removing the bearings of private reflection and self-direction? The overnight success of Trivial Pursuit seems to indicate that most of us share approximately the same body of trivia. In all this, TV may very well be doing our thinking for us—at least, the part of it which requires us to be quick and comprehensive. Though not always coming before our own thoughts, the TV may be the port of entry for individual participation in an on-going collective rumination. It may also prove to have been woman's port of entry into the public realm.

TV SCREENS

Perhaps the least-known psychological effect of television is that it has externalized both the context and the program of personal information-processing. In the psychological set-up created by literacy, our program is the alphabet. It is somehow inside, having affected in a semipermanent way the organization of our visual system. The 'frame,' on the other hand, our perspectivist organization of time and space, is outside. With television, both the frame and the program are outside. The programming works from the outside in. Even our time is minutely programmed by the TV hour. The frame, of course, is the TV screen itself. Being two-dimensional, it eliminates perspective instantly. McLuhan observed that, quite literally, there cannot be a point of view in front of TV. Besides the fact that, as with any film or video medium, the point-of-view is inescapably provided by the camera, there is also the impossibility of changing the angle of vision in front of a small two-dimensional screen. The TV screen is a rigorously prescriptive perceptual frame, because all at once it frames the dimensions of whatever there is to look at, focuses the eyes and attention of the viewer and conditions absolutely the way the information is processed and delivered.

RECOVERING AUTONOMY

However, broadcast television may have reached its maturation, if not its saturation point. In fact, broadcast TV's era probably peaked in the late sixties and early seventies, coinciding not accidentally with the Baby Boomers. During the late seventies, TV was yielding more and more control to computers. The key word here is control. Just as we were once human putty for one-way manipulation by TV, we are just now waking up to the possibility of talking back to our televisions. Besides learning to talk to our screen, thanks to the home-computer boom of the eighties, we've also been through a four-phase education program run by technology inviting us to be producers.

1. "Channel-surfing" was our beginners' course in editing.
2. Video recording and playback was our intermediate course in production.
3. Lightweight VHS and HIGH-8 technologies (including cheaper and better editing facilities) allow anybody to express themselves in movie format. A new electronic literature may be in

the making. The video camera is about to become an electronic pen.

4. With keyboards and mice, we have learned to impact the screen's information-processing properties in an interactive way.

Indeed, the quick and universal adoption of PC's can be understood as the necessary protest of the individual in a society dominated by video. The computer has partly recovered the balance between the video and alphabetic mindsets by providing a kind of electronic book. But it is precisely at this juncture that we need to reappraise our concept of the medium and its functions.

Computers allow us to "talk back" to our screens and thus introduce the second element that will lead to externalizing our consciousness. Talking back requires some form of interfacing. It is therefore understandable that much of the work that has gone into building better computers has focused on improving interfaces and making them user-friendly. Simultaneously, the interface has become the privileged locus of information processing. That's precisely where the boundary between inside and outside has started to blur. The important question haunting cognitive psychologists today is whether when using computers we are the master or the slave—or a bit of both. Are the routines of programming purely external events pertaining to an objective machine or do they impose such a rigorous protocol of operations that they turn us into mere program extensions? The only possible answer to that critical question is to recognize that computers have created a new kind of intermediate cognition, a bridge of continuous interaction, a *corpus callosum* between the outside world and our inner selves.

CHAPTER THREE

THE ALPHABETIC PROGRAM

THE ORIGINS OF TECHNOLOGY IN LANGUAGE

"For them, I invented numbers, the first among the sciences, but I also taught humans how to put letters together, memory of all things, mother of all the arts."

– Aeschylus, *Prometheus Bound*

IT IS ARGUABLE that our alphabet influences our relationship with space and time from the moment we learn to read. For example, in western visual space, the past is on the left and the future is where our writing goes, to the right. To illustrate this, look at the rectangles in Figure 1. Which line is going up and which one is going down?

 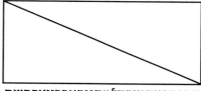

ABCDEFGHIJKLMNOPQRSTUVWXYZ   אבגדהוזחטיכדלממסננעפףצץקרשת

Figure 1

If you select the one on the left as going downwards, chances are that your principal reading medium is not the Roman alphabet. But if it is, your propensity to read from left to right, together with the drag of your right visual field, will only allow you to conclude that action, time and reality itself march from left to right.

THE INVENTION OF MONEY

Prometheus, the left-brained god, is said to have invented the Greek alphabet. But according to Aeschylus, he first invented accounting. The truth of the matter is probably that, during the earliest civilizations, the invention of writing was directly related to that of money. The following story is worth telling because the two inventions of money and writing have determined our culture for two and a half millennia.

When the American scholar Denise Schmandt-Besserat solved the mystery of the Sumerian tokens, she made one of the most interesting archaeological discoveries of recent times.[12] As a young woman travelling the sites of ancient civilizations around the eastern Mediterranean, she noticed strange little earthenware tokens in many of the local museums. The tokens were about the size of marbles. Some had the shape of an ox, a wheatsheaf or an amphora. Others were inscribed with indecipherable geometric shapes. No one knew the purpose served by these ancient clay relics, though some archaeologists thought them to be toys. The best suggestion, offered by the most enlightened local curators, was that they represented some form of money.

Following up this lead, Denise Schmandt-Besserat began to collect and classify all the tokens she could find, looking at their differences and similarities from every point of view. The first thing she discovered was that these tokens could be found on archaeological sites all over the Near and Middle East. Second, although the local variations showed marked differences, the number of basic shapes and patterns did not exceed thirty. The next discovery was that, on site, the tokens had been found originally among bits and pieces of broken pottery. At first, believing the pots to be ordinary vessels that had contained the tokens, Schmandt-Besserat did not bother to reconstitute them. She soon changed her mind, however, when she found mysterious markings on some of the fragments and later came across an unbroken vessel with the tokens at one archaeological site. This unbroken and unmarked vessel was hollow. When shaken, it appeared to contain pieces of clay. An X-ray soon confirmed Schmandt-Besserat's hypothesis that the vessel did indeed contain a few tokens.

The question was, why should such tokens be hidden from view? After re-examining the markings on some fragments of pottery, Schmandt-Besserat concluded that the rudimentary shapes on their surfaces had been made by pressing a rounded object on the clay before it had time to dry. The real significance of all this had already occurred to Schmandt-Besserat, but she determined to check every last detail before jumping to conclusions. All the tokens and the pieces of pottery found together were classified and catalogued with precise dates, locations and contexts. In the course of a few months, Schmandt-Besserat had found a large number of broken and unbroken "bullas" as she called vessels. The most important thing, however, was that some of the later bullas bore markings that corresponded exactly with the number and the shapes of the tokens they contained.

One last find would confirm Schmandt-Besserat's belief that she had not only traced the origins of "printed" money, but also the origin of writing itself. Among the later bullas, Schmandt-Besserat found flat rectangular clay tablets that bore markings similar to those found on the surface of the bullas. This indicated that if the bullas were indeed used to represent money, then the flat clay pieces were the first banknotes—a kind of Flintstone money, so to speak. Digging deeper into the ancient history of money, going back again and again to little local museums, Schmandt-Besserat found large quantities of flat tablets bearing simple geometric or symbolic markings. More chronological research led to the following conclusions:

1. At first, the tokens were used without containers to symbolize recognizable items such as sheep, wheat and oil and wine amphoræ. They would be used as promissory notes to guarantee the fairness of deals and bargains. To pay for goods or services, I would give you a couple of sheep tokens that I would promise to redeem, at some point in the future, by giving you a couple of sheep from my stock.

2. Later, the tokens were bundled in a bulla, perhaps to simplify the procedure of larger transactions, but more likely as a measure of protection against fraudulent minting of tokens. Probably, around the same time, the tokens began to take on less naturalistic and more geometric shapes, since society had accepted them as a reliable code of practice.

3. As time went on, people realized that it was not exactly convenient to have to break the bulla in order to know exactly what was inside. The solution was to mark the surface of the bullas.

4. Now, once there was a way of finding out what was inside the bullas without having to break them, why use a bulla at all? After all, one could just as easily make the same markings on some less fragile and more portable material. Hence the creation of the money tablet.

So far, so good. But what does all this have to do with the invention of writing? This is where Denise Schmandt-Besserat shows us an example of true and devoted scholarship. Someone else might have been content to answer the original question. Instead, Schmandt-Besserat went back to the drawing board and back on the archaeological trail to unravel the precise history of the money tablets themselves. Not only did she find a discernible progression in the symbolic complexity of the tables, she also found that designs from the end of the third millennium BC, in Sumer, were becoming less naturalistic and more stylized—as if the markings were no longer literal representations.

In addition, later tablets indicated numbers not by repeating a symbol, as did the earlier ones, but by joining the symbol to a particular sign showing the value or the quantity. Schmandt-Besserat went still further, to the point where the connection between money and writing can finally be established. Many of the simpler stylized shapes found on the money tablets could also be found among the earliest examples of Sumerian writings. Writings that have survived to this day.

In summary, collapsing several thousand years, this is what happened:

1. The invention of the tablets established the formula, the medium and the principle of symbolizing real things by markings.
2. The use of the tablets revealed that one could establish a reliable and distributed system of communication agreed upon by all participants in the same culture.
3. The number of transactions permitted by the system was unlimited and the various symbols for goods and services supported by the system was limited only by the imagination of the designers.
4. It must have soon occurred to users that if objects could be represented in this way, so too could language—albeit in the rudimentary pictographic code developed by Sumerians.

What followed is well-documented. The Akkadians took over the Sumerian system of stylized pictograms and adapted it to their own language. But instead of representing images and ideas, the signs were used to represent the sounds of their own language. Thus was created the first syllabary, a system known as cuneiform, which would play an important role in influencing the development of the Phoenician and later the Greek and the Roman alphabets.

Developed and refined over the five millennia, the alphabet became the most important concept ever to occupy the mind, soul and body of any human culture until the discovery of electricity. Counting and accounting are already cerebral activities—specifically, they relate to the properties of the so-called left brain. So, too, does language. It is neither surprising nor irrelevant that money and writing were invented within a common context, for they are both cultural projections of the selective biases of the left hemisphere of the brain. All writing systems, even those that make the most use of the right brain for design and decipherment, eventually lead back to left-hemisphere functions. If only because, of necessity, they lead back to language itself, a left-brain function. However, of all the writing systems invented to this day, none has emphasized more radically or more exclusively the biases of the left brain than the Greco-Roman phonetic alphabet. You and I, of course, were brought up on it.

All of which makes a good starting point. Because if you can read this, you yourself are an example of how the brain can be affected by a technology such as the phonetic alphabet.

THE ALPHABET AND THE BRAIN

Over the last ten years, scholars from various countries have been trying to determine whether or not the fact that we write to the right affects our way of thinking.[13] In other words, have the Greek and Roman alphabets had a fundamental impact on both the content and structure of our minds?

The hypothesis is that the alphabet has played a determining role in emphasizing timing and sequencing, the two core functions of the left hemisphere of the human brain. In the long run, this has led to the typically western reliance on rationality and the rationalization of all experience, including that of spatial perception.

One of the earliest and rarest suggestions of a correlation between writing and brain specialization was made by Joseph E. Bogen. "Quite possibly, some anatomical asymmetry underlies the potential for hemisphere specialization."[14] Then again, it is also clear that we develop our potential according to our environment. Although humans of any culture, so far as we know, have the innate capacity to learn to read and write, many remain illiterate and never acquire the most special of left-hemisphere functions. Conversely, we can readily comprehend the concept of a society in which "right hemisphere illiteracy" is the rule. One of the specializations of the right hemisphere is art and the inability to draw accurately is a symptom of right-hemisphere illiteracy. Although most of us can write a good description of a friend's face, few of us can draw an identifiable representation of the same friend.

The theory I proposed in *The Alphabet and the Brain: The Lateralization of Writing* is based on the observation that when the ancient Greeks created their alphabet, around the eighth century BC, they changed the direction of their written script from the left orientation of the Phoenician model to the right orientation to which we've become accustomed.[15] A few years ago, to find out if there were corresponding features between the inner structure of orthographies and their orientation on the surface of writing, I surveyed all the writing systems of the world. The results were surprising.

All writing systems that represent sounds are written horizontally, but all systems that represent images, like Chinese ideograms or Egyptian hieroglyphs, are written vertically. Furthermore, the vertical columns of image-based systems generally read right to left.

All writing systems, except for the Etruscan, are written to the right if they contain vowels. All systems without vowels are written to the left. To explain this, I had to study the brain and the visual systems.

My theory, which pertains not only to the Greek situation but also to the impact of alphabetic literacy generally, can be summarized by three basic hypotheses. Each theoretical point is supported by specific historical evidence.

1. It is the intrinsic structure of a language that determines the direction of writing. Systems such as Greek, Latin or Ethiopian, which were first modelled on right-to-left consonantal systems, eventually changed the direction of their script, but only after vowels were added to the original model.
2. The choice of direction depends on whether the reading process is based on combining letters by context (right to left) or stringing them in sequence (left to right). This is because

the typical human brain recognizes configurations faster in the left visual field, while it detects sequences faster in the right visual field. The change of direction in Greek script happened soon after a full complement of vowels was added to the exclusively consonantal Phoenician language. The presence of the vowels made the sequence of letters continuous, whereas the system from which they had borrowed was a discontinuous line of symbols, which relied upon being read in context rather than sequence.

The fact that our alphabet changed direction once it acquired vowels supports my hypothesis: that the structure of our language has put pressure on our brain to emphasize its sequential and "time-ordered" processing abilities.

Since literacy is generally acquired during our formative years, and since it affects the organization of language—our most integral information-processing system—there are good reasons to suspect that the alphabet also affects the organization of our thought. Language is the software that drives human psychology. Any technology that significantly affects language must also affect behaviour at a physical, emotional and mental level. The alphabet is like a computer program, but more powerful, more precise, more versatile and more comprehensive than any software yet written. A program designed to run the most powerful instrument in existence: the human being. The alphabet found its way in the brain to specify the routines that would support the firmware of the literate brainframe. The alphabet created two complementary revolutions: one in the brain and the other in the world.

FRAMING THE BRAIN

We write to the right not only because it's the way we've been taught, but principally because it's what our brain and our visual systems want us to do. Few people realize that our two eyes are made of four half-eyes: two for each side of the visual field. The left halves are operated by the right side of the brain, while the right halves are operated by the left side.

This is of the utmost relevance to the question of the direction of orthographies. Clinical research shows that we do not 'see' in the same way to the left as to the right. What we see to the left is literally comprehended—taken in all at once. But what we see to the right is analyzed bit by bit. This corresponds precisely to the earlier differences made between the biases of the left and the right hemispheres. In effect, the work of our eyes is divided like the work of our hands. The two left halves seize the world, and the two right cut it up into its component parts.

Lh	*Left half*
Rh	*Right Half*
F	*Visual field*
R	*Right*
L	*Left*
O	*Optic chiasm*
C	*Corpus callosum*
Rf	*Right half visual field*
Lf	*Left half visual field*
Lhs	*Left hemisphere*
Rhs	*Right hemisphere*

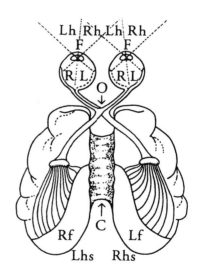

FIGURE 2

How relevant is this to the question of the alphabet? To read any writing system, you have to recognize the shape of the symbols and analyze the sequence of symbols. Depending upon which is the more urgent, shape or sequence, the writing system will go left or right. If you have to guess and cross-check the writing, it is important to see the shape first. Arabic and Hebraic readers cross-check their texts, for example, because they have to guess the unwritten vowels. For the instant survey of an entire field, our left field of vision works faster and better than the right. On the other hand, when we read Dutch or English, we first have to see the order of the letters one after the other, a task better accomplished by the right visual field. That is why our alphabet, a linear, sequential system of coded information, is written to the right. This is my primary hypothesis.

My secondary hypothesis is that learning to read and write alphabetic text will condition the basic processing routines of eye–brain co-ordination. These in turn have a feedback effect on other sensory and psychological processes. Although present methods of investigation won't allow us to go deep enough into the brain for clinical verification, one major product of the alphabetic culture can be readily demonstrated as a "frame" or mindset. It is the idea of "perspective" that features the main characteristics of the alphabetic mindset. In this way, the alphabet probably changed the way we see the world.

FRAMING THE WORLD

The most visible and, perhaps, the most important effect of the alphabetic revolution was, in my opinion, the invention of perspective. Perspective, or the art of representing space proportionally in three dimensions, is a direct projection of the literate brain. It is the inverted mirror-image of the organization of the literate consciousness. Contrary to popular opinion, there is absolutely nothing natural about perspective. It is a very contrived way of representing space. Take a look around you and you'll see that, although you can probably impose a perspectivist grid on your surroundings, nothing obliges you to do so, and nothing in what you see now proposes a vanishing point. As I am writing this, in the South of France, I am reminded of Cézanne making the same point even more forcefully, as he tried again and again to paint non-perspectivist portraits of the Montagne Sainte-Victoire behind Aix-en-Provence.

Perspective is the division of space into proportional segments. Look at the illustrations from any treatise on perspective by Alberti or Dürer, and what strikes you first is the thick network of lines joining every structure and feature. At work is a painstaking precision in measuring exactly the distances from one point to another, as if the rigorous ordering of intervals within their 'real' proportions was as important to the draughtsman as the disappearance of all converging lines into the same central vanishing point. This ubiquitous and pervasive measurement can, of course, be interpreted merely as a novice painter's guide to the proper way to render perspective.

However, there is another way to understand this manner of representing space. By showing the proportionate reduction of size and distance on paper as a decreasing vista from the viewpoint, the draughtsman is putting time into space. The artist is representing the successive order of objects in a spatial reality. However, he is not showing what is actually there, but how it ought to appear to the viewer. Indeed, he is not showing 'real space,' but space organized by a highly biased and selective vision. It is the bias of time over space. 'Real' space would show distances as they are. The bias of timing shows them within an hierarchical order of appearance, or in this case, disappearance. Why would anybody want to do that?

For us to be able to orient ourselves in life, there is no special need for a scientific or naturalistic representation of three-dimensional space. Many other perceptual properties of the visual system, even in monocular vision, contribute to our appreciation of depth-of-field. We don't really want or need to see things in perspective, unless we are required to estimate proportions in the visual field, for example, when we are driving a car. In art, in children's drawings especially, there is no necessity for perspective either. Untutored children are not concerned with drawing objects in perspective. In fact, western culture is the only one that has shown any interest in representing the world by perspective. Chinese, Egyptian and African cultures have remained largely indifferent to it. Even our own culture did not care for it during the Middle Ages. People only developed a taste for perspective during times of great pushes of alphabetization, that is, when they first learned to read the alphabet during the Golden Age of Ancient Greece and then again around the time when print was invented by Johannes Gutenberg. The discovery, first of foreshortening in Greece during the sixth and fifth centuries BC, then of perspective between the late thirteenth century and the late Renaissance, could indeed be the best examples of how the alphabet re-framed our mind.[16]

My suggestion is that the increased participation of the left hemisphere, which is required for reading our orthography, leads to a more intense collaboration of both sides of the brain to encourage and support stereo vision. We can readily appreciate how our ordinary binocular vision puts everything "in perspective," so to speak. The brain needs two eyes, looking out from two slightly different viewpoints, in order to calculate the proportions of space between objects. To achieve perspective, the brain is required to compute the ratios along with the final product of the combined visual fields of both eyes. It is principally the left hemisphere, not the right, that makes this calculation and thus analyzes the visual field. But the total process is not unilateral; it is fairly complex. As I already mentioned, our total visual field is covered by four half-eyes. This is the basis for the so-called optic chiasm. The division of each eye into two parts is critical to understanding the fundamental mechanism of vision because, although each part of the same eye is exposed to approximately the same area of vision, it does not see it in the same way.

Perspectivist vision became a privileged system of representation. Early in the Renaissance, rich patrons began to clamour for this exciting way of showing reality. It must have been almost magical for viewers to discover perspective in the great artworks of the Renaissance. The excitement came not only from the novelty but also from the concordance of what cultivated people saw in the painting and what happened within their own minds. What they were looking at was not only a model for organizing visual and spatial information, but also, and perhaps more important for them, a model for the organization of thought itself. A new order was in the making—the order of perspective.

STOPPING THE WORLD

Seeing things in perspective means putting everything into its proper place, with its right proportion in your mind. Rationality, from the Latin *ratio*, also implies the sense of proportion. Rationalism is the study of objects, notions and relationships not simply in isolation but with respect to their proportion among other things belonging to the same order. Rationality is part of the alphabetic psychodynamic and is expressed, without doubt, in the perspectivist frame.

The big problem with reality is that there is too much of it and that it is always on the move, ever changing as you try to grab it. However, the kind of reality framed by perspective was very selective and very reliable. Through the use of perspective, the alphabetic brainframe slapped the two dominant co-ordinates of time and space on reality and stopped it. Just as our natural vision divides its task between seeing an object and analyzing it, perspective as a visual strategy allowed our whole culture to hold the world in space and analyze it in time.

A story told by Michael Smart, a topographer working for the Canadian government, will serve as an illustration of how critical this exceptional managing of time and space has been for our perception of reality. Michael was working in the northern Ontario bush with an Algonquin guide, defining the features and tracing the original names of rivers, hills, valleys and other landmarks. At one point, Michael said to his guide: "Hey, we are lost!" The guide gave him a withering glance and answered: "We are not lost, the camp is lost."* In a flash, Michael realized a very important aspect of what separated his vision of the world from that of his guide: for Michael,

---

* This story has been travelling a great deal around intellectual circles in southern Ontario. I have had the privilege of hearing it twice from Michael Smart himself, the first time, in 1972, at one of the famous Monday night Culture and Technology Seminars held by McLuhan; and the second time, in February 1991, on a train from Toronto to Ottawa.

space was fixed and he was a free agent moving around in it, like an actor on a stage, a vast area in which you could lose your way. The guide, however, saw space as something within rather than outside the body, a fluid and ever-changing medium in which one could never lose one's way, where the only fixed point in the universe consisted of himself, and within which, although he might be putting one foot in front of the other, he never actually moved. There are cultures where walking is not seen as traversing space but as pushing space under one's feet.

But for us westerners, the alphabet, by emphasizing the timing properties of the brain, regulated the collaboration between the left and right hemispheres in order to stabilize and focus our approach to nature. We began to occupy and manipulate space instead of it occupying and manipulating us. No wonder that the rapid progress of literacy during the Renaissance was accompanied by equally rapid progress in the field of world exploration, geography and astronomy.

CUTTING THE WORLD: THE MASTER CODES

Because of the sequential properties of our alphabetic conditioning, the western mind has also been trained to divide information into small chunks and reassemble them in a left-right sequential order. The alphabet has supported the basic inspiration and the models for the most powerful codes of mankind: the atomic structure, the genetic string of amino acids, the computer bit. All these codes have a power of action, of creation, and they all stem from the basic model of the alphabet.

It is the literate mind-program and the alphabetic model, for example, that have directed our minds to dig deep into matter by analyzing even smaller entities, right down to the atom. The atom is just an idea—it has no physical reality, except in a transient state. Yet, even as an idea, it contains more physical power than anything concrete invented by man. The idea of the atom was discovered by

Democritus of Abdera in the fifth century BC. Without the slightest shred of evidence, he came to his conclusion that the elements of matter must be like the indivisible phonemes of the alphabet, thus inventing the very notion that one day in 1945 threatened to destroy the world. The hidden ground of this discovery is, however, not the clever poetic mind of Democritus, who happened to chance upon a convenient metaphor, but rather the deeply ingrained divisional principle wedged in the recesses of the educated Greek mind and hence in our own minds—the alphabet.

The genetic code itself, the code of life, is a primitive kind of alphabetic structure of four amino acids combined in various ways to form extended strings. Genetic engineering is effected with what is called recombinant DNA, a kind of "rewriting" of the original genetic structure. New forms of life are created by borrowing information from one cell and placing it in another belonging to a different species. The information thus lifted from its context is called "messenger RNA." Anything written with the alphabet is like messenger RNA—undiluted information with no living context. The secret of inventing and innovating is lifting information from one context and placing it in another. That is why the alphabet is the only system of writing in the whole world that, soon after its creation, changed the orientation of human culture from tradition—looking to the past for models of behaviour—to innovation, forever projecting into the future, the elusive resolution of humanity's problem-ridden inventions.

THE "LITERATE DYE"

Thanks to the program installed in our heads by the alphabet, we have invented or greatly refined history, geography, grammar, law, philosophy, physics, geometry, astronomy, art, architecture and practically all branches of knowledge. As Paul Levinson wrote so elegantly: "The addition of a drop of blue dye to a glass of water results not in blue dye plus water, but in blue water: a new reality."[17] As

McLuhan and others have often pointed out, the inculcation of the habit of literacy results not in a pre-literate world plus readers, but in a literate world: a new world in which everything is seen through the eyes of literacy.

CHAPTER FOUR

CYBERSPACE

"The future is already here, it's just that it hasn't been evenly distributed."

— William Gibson

REALITIES THAT MONEY CAN BUY

N *Total Recall,* a film that capitalized on our new-found interest in virtual reality* and science-fiction technologies, Arnold Schwarzenegger woke up in a sweat. He didn't know whether he was waking into or waking out of a total fantasy, manufactured for him by a drug-based travel agency. Because his rebuilt memories were so real, he couldn't tell fact from fiction.

Sooner or later, this could happen to you, except that you wouldn't have to wake up in a sweat and you wouldn't be dreaming. In order to stop the experience, you would simply have to remove your eyephones and turn off the computer.

---

* Just as AI universally stands for "artificial intelligence," "virtual reality" is henceforth sufficiently current as to be designated as VR. But virtual reality could just as well have been called artificial imagination or artificial consciousness. It is because we can now include such sensory inputs as artificial vision, hearing and touching into our extended sensorium that we can truly consider the possibility of artificial consciousness. AI is really AC minus the interplay of the senses. It is only by adding the sensory interplay that we can reconstitute outside our body the kind of interiority that is characteristic of human consciousness.

The realities that money can buy are not made in Hollywood but at a growing number of research labs such as the Head Mounted Display research centre at the University of Chapel Hill, North Carolina, or the Human Interface Technology Lab in Seattle. With virtual reality machines such as Jaron Lanier's RB-2 (Reality Built for Two), you don't merely watch the dream unfold in front of you, you walk right into it and actually meet other people there. This even goes one better than the "participactive" video-screen game in Ray Bradbury's *Fahrenheit 451*. Meanwhile, should you prefer the world of work to the dream world of play, there are a growing number of professional applications. "Using a treadmill and steerable handlebars, architects and engineers can navigate through a virtual building, as seen through a head mounted display."[18] Developers, architects, town planners and real estate firms are already using virtual reality walk-throughs to sell unbuilt houses and condominiums. Virtual reality machines make literal the fact that for some cultures, walking is not seen as traversing space but as "pushing space under one's feet."

INTEGRATION

In real terms, of course, VR is still some way from *Total Recall*'s substitute universe. The present hurdle for computing is insufficient power: currently, we're unable to produce high-definition video image changers in real time. As a result VR displays are slightly jerky and cartoonish. But today's prototypes light the way. Such developments are in progress in computer technology and every other technology seems to be converging upon virtual reality. Electrotechnology is beginning to feed back on itself, breeding new technologies.

If, in its early beginnings, electrification was applied on a first come first served basis, computerization is now looking more and more like a biological growth spurt. Artificial Intelligence, Expert Systems and Neural Networks are invading all media, integrating electronic technologies via universal digitization for the convergence of audio, video, telecommunications and computer technologies. We talk now about digitization as if it were a new thing, but it goes back to the origins of alphabetic writing that cuts reality into letters that have no meaning by themselves. Digitization itself has a history: the translation from the alphabet to electricity was effected first for the telegraph. Samuel Morse reduced the twenty-six variables of the alphabet to a code of three variables: long, short, no signal. Computer engineers further reduced the three signals to a code of two: on/off. However, just as subatomic particles divide the atom, digitization cuts into language well beyond its natural divisions.

Today, we are witnessing a three-level integration of technologies.

1. INNER. Hyper-concentration and acceleration of computing power.
2. OUTER. Standardization for international telecommunication networks.
3. INTERACTIVE. Biological interactivity between humans and machine in VR.

Should VR capture the imagination before it has proved itself, it is because, more than any other technological breakthrough, it typifies the trend towards integration. Here is a quick run-through of some of the current high-tech developments leading us towards VR.

- real-time processing with UHSI and ULSI (ultra-high speed and ultra-large-scale integration)
- fifth generation computers: single chip memories with computer-assisted design capability, parallel processing, powerful software, vision systems and voice recognition
- miniaturization and integration of head-gear and motion sensor devices
- high definition TV screen and pixel technology
- neural networks and parallel processing
- high-end robotics

- flight simulation.
- tactile micro-sensor technology integrated into datasuits
- artificial vision and other sensory simulations
- 3-D interface technologies
- fibre-optic technologies and optic switches
- 3-D sound encryption

By putting our physical bodies inside our extended nervous system, by means of electric media, we set up a dynamic by which all previous technologies that are mere extensions of hands and feet and teeth and bodily heat-controls—all such extensions of our bodies including cities—will be translated into information systems.

– Marshall McLuhan[19]

Virtual reality was foreseen, in this passage, some three decades before the idea was even considered. McLuhan did not need to see a system to know that the purpose of computerization was to turn hardware into software, to hand over the reins of physical power to thought. Indeed, if we take the concept to its ultimate conclusion, we discover that the purpose of VR is to command external psychological simulations by thought alone.

APPLICATIONS

Popular reaction to VR demonstrations—or just to the idea of VR—range from "It's the biggest thing in cultural transformation since the printing press" (Howard Rheingold, *Whole Earth Review*[20]), or "It will kill television" (Jaron Lanier) or "It will allow corporate America to survive and expand" (Steve Pruitt and Tom Barrett[21]) to "Another technology from which the users will probably profit more than its purveyors" (Esther Dyson, *Forbes Magazine*[22]) and "Sure, but what's it really good for?" (Joe Public). John Perry Barlow, VR poet and one-time lyricist for the Grateful Dead, rightly observes that "the presence of such unclaimed vastness seems to elicit territorial impulses from psychic regions too old to recognize the true infinity of this new frontier."[23] VR either shocks you into recognizing that we have just stepped up our collective brainpower or it leaves you cold. Meanwhile, there are those who are warming to the idea of turning virtual realities into very real income.

Simple applications such as computer-assisted analysis and design are already practised by Ford, Chrysler et al. VR saves money and time in substituting for clay models of car prototypes and, as Esther Dyson remarks, "you can sit and adjust your seat level inside the fictitious car."[24] But strange new concepts such as Cyberspace, Autodesk's name for its brand of VR research and development, or Corporate Virtual Workspace (CVW) and Personal Virtual Workspace (PVW) are beginning to filter into the corporate consciousness. Steve Pruitt and Tom Barrett predict that corporations of the future may only exist in cyberspace, carving up market niches in a hyper-competitive technological marketplace without head offices anywhere except on-line.[25]

In more concrete terms, we have seen that industry is already experimenting with "walk-through" models of architectural and urban plans. Some people claim that Atlanta won the competition to hold the 1996 Olympics because it included a VR walk-through simulation of the planned stadium and grounds in its presentation. Work is also progressing on many medical applications, notably at the University of North Carolina. For example, researcher Jim Chung uses eyephones and 3-D graphics to move inside simulations of a patient's body. This is how Marc de Groot describes it:

> Suppose you are a brain surgeon, scheduled to perform an operation to remove a tumor. The tumor's position in the brain makes its removal risky. To decide how best to proceed, you and a fellow doctor each don the [VR] goggles, which provide you with a three-dimensional model of the patient's brain. You use your vantage point inside the body to examine the tumor's position

from otherwise impossible angles. . . . With this new mode of visualization, a doctor will be able to place computer simulated radiation sources so that the tumor can be irradiated evenly with minimal damage to the surrounding tissue." [26]

Howard Rheingold also suggests that 3-D visualization may be the only way to overcome the complexity of certain scientific/technological fields such as molecular innovation. Indeed, VR's destiny may be to transfer some of the bulk of cognition from vision to touch in another UNC application described here by Marc de Groot:

> VR technology allows scientists to see complex molecules in 3-D with full depth perception, and permits them to "walk around" the molecules, to examine them from a variety of angles. Research is underway at UNC to develop the means by which scientists can "pick up" and manipulate the molecules they are analyzing. For example, UNC researchers are using a special I/O device called a force-feedback arm. A scientist puts his arm into this device, which resembles an enormous, shoulder-length, metal glove with pulleys. The device senses the position of the scientist's arm and hand to make him feel that an object in the virtual world is pressing against him. With this tool the scientist can "hold" a molecule in his hand and position it against another molecular surface while he watches and feels how well the two bind chemically. The computer and force-feedback arm actually simulate the tug of the electrons as the atoms rub against one another. [27]

Having tested the installation at UNC, Rheingold testifies that "the arm has enough force to tire your arm if you actively wrestle with a molecule for many minutes. . . . I tried to twist, rotate, jam, tweak, and frob the thing into place by looking at the 3-D jigsaw puzzle on the screen and manipulating it with my hand. It didn't take any time at all to develop a sense that I was actually feeling a molecule 'out there' in the space defined by the screen" [28]

INTEGRATION IS TOUCH

Integration is a word that means at least two things. The first, every-body knows, is making whole or putting things together in their proper way. The word was also used by nineteenth-century econo-mists to indicate the process by which subsidiary activities were related to main industries. However, the word's much older mean-ing is related to the Latin *tangere*, which means 'to touch.' Not only that, it means specifically 'to touch from within'—its most interest-ing and relevant sense.

A few VR researchers are especially interested in creating believ-able simulations of touch. This is no accident. Not only is touch the ground of reality, it is also one of the bases of understanding and comprehension. Subliminally, intellectual operations are tactile experiences. Even AI researchers recognize that true information processing should not be restricted to logical operations, but must include the senses. What VR brings to this trend is a means to project our nervous system electronically, and especially the electronic extension of touch.[29]

As St. Thomas made abundantly clear, sharing a vision isn't quite the same as being able to touch it. In spite of its current shortcom-ings, the simulation of touch in VR is more powerful than that of vi-sion because of the supporting 3-D. People think of 3-D as visual, but the dominant sensation of 3-D is tactile. When you walk around in VR, your whole body is in touch with your surroundings, as it is with water when you are in a swimming pool. As Jaron Lanier suggests of virtual worlds, "the entire universe is your body and physics is your language."[30] The message of 3-D is penetration and depth, not just the perspectivist angle of vision. Indeed, the story of computer stimula-tion is one of gradual penetration into a tactile environment. From 2-D to 3-D, then to the rapid development of tactile and force-feedback sensations, we are being sucked into a richly textured electronic vortex.

The call of electro-tactile technology reminds me of the myth of Ulysses' sirens, with their intensely erotic connotations. VR is like a siren that drags us into a sea of electrons. Within our rather intellectual abstract tradition, we have tended to ignore and even to fear the rich learning experience derived from touch. In fact, we were terrified of touch until the sixties, when television induced a collective craving for the recovery of bodies lost to literate heads. After a rash of touch-ins and feel-ins spread eastward from California, we began to settle down to a more comfortable relationship with our bodies. But we never gave touch its honoured position among our principal sensory modes. VR is about to change all that.

It has occurred to educators and to many artists that touch may be our most important cognitive tool. Babies learn by touching, adults learn by "grasping" a situation—a tactile metaphor. We develop a kind of gut feel for the things we know or need to know. In the very early years of corporate mainframe computers, McLuhan's own artistic sensibility led him to conclude that computerization would lead to touch:

> Our very word "grasp" or "apprehension" points to the process of getting at one thing through another, of handling and sensing many facets at a time through more than one sense at a time. It begins to be evident that "touch" is not the skin but the interplay of the senses, and "keeping in touch" or "getting in touch" is a matter of a fruitful meeting of the senses, of sight translated into sound and sound into movement and taste and smell. The "common sense" was, for many centuries held to be the peculiar human power of translating one kind of experience of one sense into all the senses, and presenting the result continuously as a unified image to the mind. In fact, this image of a unified ratio among the senses was long held to be the mark of our rationality, and may in the computer age easily become so again. For it is now possible to program ratios among the senses that approach the condition of consciousness.[31]

Thus a virtual "reality" is one that you can touch and feel, as well as see and hear with your real senses—not just your mind's eye or ear. We can now add the "mind's hand" to our thinking. Indeed, by penetrating the screen with the Dataglove, our real hand turns into a technical metaphor, making tangible things that before were merely visible. We may henceforth want to feel the content of our thought. But before the invention of VR, no one conceived of a "mind's hand." The concept did not present itself. There seemed to be no special need for feeling the objects we carried in our minds. Today, the inclusion of touch among our other techno-sensorial and psycho-technical extensions may inspire us or our children to change our minds about how we make up our minds.

CYBERSPACE

Until recently we couldn't just think of something and get it done, magically, on the spot. Changes to a written page or a painted canvas would take minutes at least. Now, the speed of interaction has increased to immediacy. It's possible to experience instant reactions— not only in VR simulations, but also with simpler eye-tracking interface devices or bio-feedback through analyzers. The technologically extended brain projects its network of intelligent sensors outside, to swallow the environment, in the same way sea cucumbers project their stomachs to capture plankton. The role of tactile extension is fundamental here because it is intimate. Tactility is involved with thought whether in our minds or in our machines, as a participant in the thinking process. Simulated tactility is the first psychotechnology powerful enough to yank us out of the literate, theoretical, frontal mindset.

Among other applications for VR, Laura Carrabine, Assistant Editor of *Computer-Aided Engineering*, quite innocently described the Flying Mouse, a new kind of program from SimGraphics, that brings us very close to cyberbrain.

Flying Mouse [is] a hand-held 3-D input device for the [Automated Airframe Assembly] program's manufacturing simulation and for creating motion paths in assembling terrain, navigating through 3-D analysis "fields," 3-D object digitizing, and applications involving 3-D object or entity positioning and viewing. The device controls the engineer's view and selects a part to test for manufacturability by moving the part though a 3-D database of sub-assemblies and checking for clearances. Since the technology allows arbitrary part motion and view alteration, real world operations can be performed. Some of these advanced CAD functions include real-time collision detection, part penetration prevention, and 3-D snap-to assemblies.[32]

The upshot of this rather forbidding high-tech talk is that, with real-time 3-D object manipulation, thinking and processing are becoming one and the same thing. If, by analogy, you can transpose the above into a child's learning environment you will have shot right through the print-oriented barrier. One person who has done just that is John Perry Barlow. Commenting on the clumsiness of our standard computer screens, he notes that the "metaphorical desktop remains flat as paper. There is none of the depth or actual spatiality of experience." He adds:

> This is not the way the mind stores information. One doesn't remember the names of his friends alphabetically. When looking for a phrase in a book, you are more likely to look for its spatial position on the page than its intellectual position in context.[33]

The point is precisely that VR will eventually allow us to store information in the way the mind stores it, and possibly teach the mind a thing or two to boot.

SIMULTANEOUS SHARED CONSCIOUSNESS

According to Jaron Lanier, "the essence of virtual reality is that it shares." He proposes that VR is the "first new level of objectively shared reality available to humanity since [the invention of] the physical world."34 While our ordinary consciousness is like processing virtual reality within a single mind, VR technology would allow many minds to collectively process a kind of "group consciousness." However, before we get there, our interface technologies will have to come much closer to the body and to the source of our thoughts.

THE GRADUAL
REMOVAL OF INTERFACES

Eric Gullichsen observes that VR goes way beyond conventional computers that are merely interactive. "A cyberspace system is dynamic: the virtual world changes in real time, both autonomously and fluidly in response to the actions of the patron. Action is visceral, and there need be no veneer of symbolic 'interface,' since the objects in this 3-D world can be directly manipulated."35 In the same publication, albeit rather uncritically, Luis Racionero suggests that the way of the future is to connect electronic pathways directly to our biological neural networks by some bionic engineering already under development.36 The idea is to remove the interfaces to achieve direct contact, so as to 'mainline' thought directly, as in real-life situation:

> We obtain raw, direct information in the process of interacting with the situations we encounter. Rarely intensive, direct experience has the advantage of coming through the totality of our internal processes—conscious, unconscious, visceral and mental—and is most completely tested and evaluated by our nature. Processed, digested, abstracted second-hand knowledge is often more generalized and concentrated, but usually affects us only intellectually—lacking the balance and completeness of experienced simulations. Although we are existing more and more in the realms of abstract, generalized concepts and principles,

our roots are in direct experience on many levels, as is most of our ability to consciously and unconsciously evaluate information.[37]

Everyone can remember their first eerie impression of intimacy created by headphones. We have become so accustomed to the Walkman that we cease to notice how the sound penetrates the whole body. Imagine a similar sensation of immediacy coming from a visual stimulation. The machine that allows for this kind of experience is already on the market. Cyberspace Corporation produces a head-band mounted eye-piece that flashes images directly onto the user's retina. The image appears to hover in the air, full-sized and exclusively for the benefit of the user. New devices: eye-tracking, image-contact and brain-wave interfaces, along with laser-to-retina projections, are moving in the general direction of immediate processing from thought to machine. Considering all the work going into this technology and the current advances in computing, we can expect shortly to have access to any mode of interface, even for the briefest span of attention.

A THINK TANK WHERE THE TANK DOES THE THINKING

Scott Fisher suggests that by giving people instant access to "greater than one viewpoint of a given scene," virtual reality "allows them to synthesize a strong visual percept from many points of view; the availability of multiple points of view places an object in context and thereby animates its meaning."[38] This, of course, was the point of Cubism, but never before have we been in a situation where several different points of view, issuing from different people, can simultaneously interact through a direct relationship to a common object of study. In the case of two people engaging in creating a common VR, such as in Jaron Lanier's primitive but impressive RB-2, these agents remain operative, but the effect is cognitive, reflecting the combined thoughts of two cognitive agents. The experience is automatically recorded in 3-D and can be replayed for new insights. Add to such a possibility that of touching the object of perception and modifying it, in selected ways ruled by selected routines, and you will eventually get the most powerful thinking machine ever devised: a think tank where the thought is the tank.

We can envisage the future of problem-solving as a vr extension of the think tank. Working out a solution to a given problem will be enhanced by simulating a complete thought-process environment, generated by the combined thinking of people regarding a single object under consideration. Eventually, we will be instantly creating new objects by thought alone, in a collaborative manner. They will be blueprints recorded for instant automated hardware production.

The most important psychological change in the long run may be that, even as we begin to explore external tactile perceptions in our extended thought processes, our personal, ordinary internalized consciousness will itself become externalized. The whole external world will become an extension of our consciousness, just as it used to be for the most "primitive" cultures of the planet. This spells not the end, but the removal of *Homo theoreticus* from centre stage, to be replaced by *Homo participans*.

CHAPTER FIVE

ROADSIDE ROMANCE

TELEVISION GETS MARRIED TO THE COMPUTER ON THE ELECTRONIC HIGHWAY

THE NEW MEDIA CONTEXT

E VEN the slowest government bureaucracies are waking up to the idea that the so-called "electronic superhighways" are just as critical to their survival as the upkeep of real highways and streets, if not more so. This realization comes from obvious factors as well as less conspicuous ones. The obvious ones are economic: for example, anybody can observe that television has ruled the mind and the marketable reality of most of the world since the early sixties. The rapid growth of personal computers since the early eighties has demonstrated that the screen could also be the focus of endless variations of domestic products and perhaps rival the auto industry for the support of national economies.

CONVERGENCE

While television and video technologies, taking their cue from photography and cinema, are primarily concerned with the conquest of our mental space, computer networks emphasize the mastery of time inherent in the telegraphic and telephone systems. The role of television is to introduce a focused, collective information-processing device into everybody's home. By adding the visual component to the existing radio network's base, TV, though still a one-way medium, installs a kind of active collective memory in the culture. TV extends private thought into the collective realm by reproducing on an external screen the main sensory combinations that we use to make sense internally. Especially when used for live broadcast, TV supplies a common referent supplemented by three key sensory inputs: hearing, sight and kinesthetic proprioception (our ability to know the position of our bodies without looking). Within a relatively short time of its technical development period, TV has manifested its latent tendency to bring the spectator into the scene of the action. Today's TV accomplishes this by offering an increasing number of interactive options from humble remote control to video recording, video editing and videoconferencing. Such developments herald the democratization of the medium. The trend from broadcasting to narrowcasting and, finally to direct input from the viewer is still being worked on in technologies such as set-top boxes and "telecomputers."

TELECOMPUTERS

It is instructive to understand the development of computers not in opposition to but in continuity with TV. In the new buzzword, "telecomputer," both the idea of "vision" and even that of "television" have disappeared. The key word of telecomputer is *tele*, a distance connecting device, like the telephone. What emerges from this term is the notion of telecommunications combined with computers. This is because, very soon, in our digital, full service, networked information environments, the entire realm of television will be swallowed by computers. Take High Definition Television

(HDTV), for example, an innovation that has less to do with definition than with digitization. HDTV is television graduating to the status of computers. Indeed, computers now linked by telephones inherit TV's most precious legacy, namely its access to large numbers of people at once in real time. However, with telecomputers, people can actually talk to each other, they can get in on the act. Whatever was dumb about TV becomes extremely intelligent on the telecomputer.

Not so evident is the combined psychological appeal of the technologies themselves: while television has always been perceived as a broadcast medium, with a largely public character, computers were personalized as stand-alone, private media. While TV provided a kind of collective mind for everybody, but with no individual input, computers were private minds without collective inputs. Convergence offers a new, unprecedented possibility, that of plugging individuals and their special needs into collective minds. This new situation is profoundly empowering; it has social and political as well as economic repercussions. It will accelerate changes and adaptations in the geopolitical scene as well as in the private sensibility of everybody. It will bring on new forms of consciousness and put new pressures on the world's educational systems to cope with the change. It will also take most markets by surprise. Indeed, while it is obvious that, short of a major political or social catastrophe, the globalization of the world will take that route, it is not quite so clear what we are going to do with all this communication power. How do you change the habit of relying on the automobile for power, action and prestige to the adoption of "telepresence" as a way of being?

NETWORKS

The recent tendency of computers to become networked is another key to the new feeling, the incipient psychology of the developing convergence. Suddenly, the telephone networks and the telecommunication companies that were powerful and effective but usually ignored by public and private sector concerns are coming to the front of our collective consciousness. Cable companies in North America are vying with the telecommunications companies to offer multimedia services, videoconferencing and video-on-demand by compressed and digitized signals. Nets, internets and ethernets are growing in rapid spurts like the brain of an infant leviathan.

THE INTERNET, TODAY'S BEST EXAMPLE OF THE "ELECTRONIC HIGHWAY"

The Internet is a network of networks that allows very precise narrowcasting and puts the control in the hands of the user. The Net is not invasive, even less so than the telephone, because it doesn't call you, you call it. Also, you can access the Net through cellular technology. Digitized data doesn't have to come down a pipe. With forty million users in over ninety countries, the number of Net users doubles every ten months. It is also capable, when connected directly to fibre or main trunks, of providing hypermedia interactivity, with networked multimedia developing very quickly: the World Wide Web.* Users pay for what they ask for, and can get directly to the source without having to clear fee-levying gateway keepers.

The Net is a monumental computer all by itself, with astounding organic memory banks and parallel processors today numbering over twenty million, tomorrow a billion coprocessors. Why would

---

* This is the name of a system that interconnects various databases on the Internet by specialized links to access information automatically. It is coupled with "browser" software, such as Mosaic, Cello or Netscape, to allow people to navigate in this electronic maze with the addition of colour, sound and motion (albeit limited). The World Wide Web has added to the seduction of the Net; the urge to get on it is growing faster than the supply of lines and equipment.

anyone want to call that a highway? The Internet is really a brain, a collective, living brain clicking as you read. It is a brain that never ceases to work, to think, to produce information, to sort and to combine. The main issue of the Net is how to plug into it and how to navigate in it. That is still a problem for many would-be users. We go at it with our TV-generation minds looking for colour and movement and instant gratification, and finding grey, dry, bookish and slow data. But the times are still changing. The Internet is going hyper and is about to provide us with the first real, on-line multimedia with World Wide Web full-colour and fully interactive services for those who can connect to it directly on main trunk lines. In more ways than one, the Internet has beat all the super highway hype by a large measure. And it comes from below, from the underground, the subconscious level of our collective intelligence. Just like the subconscious level, it is made of way too much data for all of it to be filtered at the conscious level. This is why larger units of processing and distributing are necessary.

BANDWIDTH

Just as they eventually became wired for the telephone, private homes as well as public offices are about to be wired for full-data and video bandwidth. There are presently many different standards and capacities that include many different telecom networks such as Integrated Services Digital Networks (ISDN). In some countries, but not all, a fair proportion of cabling can carry up to 900 million bits per second but is not yet switched for digitization nor wired for interactive response. Governments and local industries are considering the options of incrementally going from standard analog lines, to digitized lines that can carry about 64,000 bits per second, to what the industry calls T3 lines, with a capacity of 45 million bits per second. This capacity would allow fully interactive transmission of data, sound, images and video. However, even as decisions are being taken in ministries and industry, breakthroughs in technology, such as asynchronous transfer mode (ATM)* that allows full-motion video to be sent on standard telephone lines, will change the rules of the game.

The question is further complicated by the fact that the wires and the airwaves are not alone anymore in vying to provide us with a conduit to collective mental processes. Cable networks generate their own brands of markets. Wired networks are different from airwaves because their image, and consequently their effects, is much closer to that of the human nervous system extended from the individual body to the social body. Broadcasting in the airwaves creates a soft, light and vibratory environment that resembles our minds more than our nerves. With the rapidly growing cellular technologies, yet another kind of relationship between individuals and public space is developing. These three simultaneous universes of communication are more or less self-organizing (when they are not battling each other and obsolete government regulations) as they discover and refine their own character and discover their optional applications. MIT guru and Media Lab Director Nicholas Negroponte says that TV and radio should move out of the airwaves altogether and leave the airspace for cellular communications that are more urgent: "Within 20 years, it will be perverse, if not illegal, to use satellites for broadcast television."[39] He may be right: there is nothing worse than a foggy brain when there is an emergency. TV and radio are part of the white noise that is needed for an organism to survive, but they don't have to monopolize the front stage of our collective consciousness all the time.

---

* In a surprising continuation of a major distinction in radio technology, assymmetrical digital subscriber loop (ADSL) and ATM seem to share some characteristics of AM and FM processing differences: while AM (amplitude modulation) affects the forms by modulating the amplitude of the sound waves, FM (frequency modulation) addresses the number or the frequency of the waves to structure and distribute the signal; likewise ADSL seems to be based on compressing the structure of the signal, while ATM is concerned with breaking down, managing and rebuilding the segments of any given signal.

RADICAL DECENTRALIZATION

With the number of different initiatives in the technical, industrial, legal and political realms, it is not easy to predict where all this activity is leading and what a stabilized technological environment might look like. With video-on-demand looming rapidly on the horizon, the public communications scene is turning private and looking more and more like telecommunications and less and less like broadcasting. George Gilder predicts the rapid demise of broadcasting in the world of electronic highways and the rise of widely available and inexpensive communications that will turn the whole relationship around: "Television and telephone systems—designed for a world in which spectrum or bandwidth was scarce—are utterly unsuited for a world in which bandwidth is abundant. The key strategy of both systems has been to centralize intelligence in local central offices, cellular base stations, cable television nodes, and broadcast centers, and give the user a stripped-down commodity terminal, whether a telephone or television set." Gilder adds that "Over the next decade, engineers will use bandwidth and computer power on the edges of networks as a substitute for switching and intelligence at the center." And he concludes that "first to fall will be the broadcast system of a few thousand stations and a few networks serving millions of idiot boxes."[40]

PAY-PER-BIT

Ideally people will be able to choose—and pay for—how much bandwidth and how many bits (that is, units of information per second) they need, at any time, in the course of their communications. This is called the "pay-per-bit" or "bandwidth-on-demand" marketing that appeals to the more enlightened critics as the most democratic and the most economically efficient way of wiring the country. Viewers and listeners will buy the time and the items they need in a "pay-per-bit" addressable database network of networks. They will also pay-per-bit and per-point for any casting they care to do. As Mitch Kapor urged in a recent issue of *Wired*, the most logical system is an open architecture, universally digitized network (improving gradually over the next fifteen years), and self-adjusting level-gauging for different capacities ranging from 64Kbs on copper wires to terabits in fibre.

MARKET IMPLICATIONS OF UNIVERSAL ACCESS

If information is truly the staple of today's economy, it might be useful to keep in mind that information is the only substance that actually grows with use, rather than depleting like our natural resources. We are looking at an economy of abundance. This economy will only occur when the infrastructure allows universal access. Universal access itself will come by nature or by force, the sooner, the better. However, it may take a political and social revolution. Just as the old monarchic power structures had to be toppled over and literally "beheaded" to make room for the body of the people in the democratic process, the present establishment of communications and information control may have to be zapped out of existence. The transition has begun quite peacefully thanks to the increased sophistication of domestic production technologies and the increased need for production.

The shift of controls from the producer/broadcaster to the consumer/user will turn a sizable minority of users into becoming their own producers, or 'prosumers.' The decentralizing of broadcasting will be accompanied by the decentralizing of production technology. As the prices go down on video and computer equipment, the quality and performance go up. It is possible today to do a better job with a semi-professional HI-8 camcorder and a computer-assisted desktop video editor with a simple sound-mixing table, than with what used to require huge editing rooms and long time delays. Transmitter technology, spurred by cellular networks, will also put broadcasting power in the hands of individuals over larger and larger areas.

FROM "COUCH POTATOES" TO "COUCH GUERRILLAS"

The deeper reason why the market will support such developments in spite of the threats they pose to established broadcasters is that the multiplication of channels via satellite, cable, telephone compression and cellular transmission will require more and more content, implying that ordinary people, even "couch potatoes" will have to contribute to content themselves. People will develop their own regular network, for business or for pleasure, without restrictions of time or place. Video-on-demand (VOD) is today's biggest future market commodity because people understand what it means, not just the end of having to rent from video stores, but a host of other services. However, by the time that VOD is in place, the bigger business item will be networked multimedia. When the problems of copyright for multimedia content are resolved—a very long shot unless rights are levied automatically—interactivity will turn many info-consumers into info-providers and create a flurry of special interest markets and attendant transnational communities.

VIDEOCONFERENCING

Quality videoconferencing with large and comfortable screens will come down in price over the next two years to $500 a session and even less later; some will still connect to standard analogue lines (perhaps with a special card added to convertible TV sets) but most will take advantage of improved compression ratios, capitalizing on competitive advances and lower prices on digitally switched, twisted-pair copper wires and, wherever applicable, early fibre networks. At first, videoconferencing will remain more popular in business, government

and academe than in the private home where many people will resent
it as an invasion of privacy and not see its advantage for cutting down
on commuting. Later, videoconferencing will create an enormous live
sex video market and simplify display room salesmanship. Portable
cellular videoconferencing (developed and distributed increasingly
from two to five years from now) will accelerate the real estate market allowing people to visit any place from their residence. Videoconferencing will multiply conditions and opportunities for public
surveys, unobtrusive polling and, alas, for fraud and police surveil-
lance. Overall, its most important effect will be to change
home/workplace relationships more radically than the automobile
did the average North American city. People will spend long periods
of time far away from their place of business, preferably in the comfort and peace of their secondary residence, their country homes.
Commuters will go back to trains because they will favour the freedom of movement needed to control an intelligent machine, say a
hand-held computer or a cellular telephone, over the control of a
dumb machine, an automobile. Architecture and development will
begin to plan and design in terms of communications accessibility
rather than in terms of roadway and hydro infrastructures.

INTERACTIVE ADVERTISING

Advertising was really given a tremendous boost by mass media, and
it supported economies of scale during the heyday of broadcast television. It is bound, at first, to suffer from the decentralization at
hand. Nobody knows quite how to make computer network users
pay in any way other than charging for the lines and for the time of
use. However, interactive multimedia, even the rather limited kind
of interactivity allowed today on some cable-borne TV, such as Montreal's Videoway system on Videotron, show the direction of things
to come. People actually like advertising and many stay up late at
night in front of their TV sets just to watch "info-mercials." Even
more, they would like to get "into" their ad, by selecting the process

and the kind of information they are presented. Furthermore, they will have a chance to respond directly to the supplier. Instead of a "mass" market of one-way communications looking for large demographics, there will be a "speed" market with two-way interactive feedforward and feedback.

Another major development is the developing possibility of finding out and recording the exact numbers of users and buyers for any product. All digital technologies converge to numbers with the greatest exactitude. There was a time in the market when you could fool most of the people, most of the time. Today, an advertiser or a corporation cannot make any false claim about the real audience or the contents of the package: in electronic conditions, you cannot fool anybody, anytime. In terms of how the human nervous system works, it makes much more sense to privilege communications that allow instant feedback on connections rather than spray gunning reality with pellets of news, ads and services.*

"WE ARE IN DESPERATE NEED OF FILTERS"

If the previous economy of the print and electronic mass media was based on production, the new economy of interactive media will be based on 'reduction,' following the image of the brain, which some neurobiologists say is not a producing mechanism, but a sort of huge reducing valve to allow ordered operations to take place in the body. Remarking upon the bewildering opportunities presented by the flexibility of computer programming, Toronto computer artist-engineer David Rokeby said, "We are in desperate need of filters."[41]

---

* The earliest example I have seen of this new direction in advertising is Volvo's contribution to *HotWired,* the on-line sister magazine of *Wired.* You can now see your potential car from several angles on-line; tomorrow, you will be driving it on a simulated highway of your choice. Of course, tomorrow, that could very well be all the driving you care to do. . . .

The jobs of the future will go to gatekeepers, intelligent assistants, information-hounds trained on the latest info about this or that. The big engineering contracts will go to encryption software for privacy and to the development of Personal Digital Assistant packages and devices to bring up instantly what you need at voice command. New forms of collective intelligence will develop based on constantly self-updating statistical samplings, such as those that can already be obtained on the Internet about the interest group's concerns and activities. They will be tuned to individual needs by keyword, inverted index searches and neurally networked integrators.

THE VALUE OF IGNORANCE

When everything is known somewhere by someone, and that information is accessible for a price, you develop a "just-in-time" kind of psychology. Why bother learning all this stuff yourself if you have access to it when you need it? Quite the reverse, you might find value in not knowing something, as the very process of discovering anything may be more useful and exciting than the content of the discovery. With real expert systems, improved by sophisticated neural networks with rapid learning curves, you don't need to be an expert in anything. Your best resource might well become your own ignorance forcing your attention to reposition itself to learn what you need from the unique angle of a non-expert. We might all develop a taste and pride for the exact recognition and avowal of our limits and limitations.

Our whole value system is now in the process of changing from hierarchical, competitive, aggression-based criteria of excellence to supportive, collaborative, interactive ones. In that new context, what will be needed more than ever will be good judgement, and that comes from experience, not learning. Judgement is like intuition, part meaning, part feeling, arising from the collaboration of mind and body in synergy.

THE BOTTOM LINE: THE
POOR PERSON'S CREDIT LINE

However, for business-minded people, all the above may just sound like sentimental stuff. In a world of plenty, how long will we find it useful to reduce everything to a single numerical evaluation and call it satisfying? Money, as it operates today, is simply not fast or complex enough to act as a proper evaluation mechanism. Indeed, as it migrates to digital convergence in purely electronic financial transactions, the nature of money itself is changing. When money reaches the speed of light it becomes pure energy. It may not need to go through a symbolic stage at all. If we follow the trend of encryption technology, we can see that it will soon be easier to attach a quantitative measurement to all operations on the global common carrier than to manage and store material representation of value. The job of money will be confined precisely to the function of parsing the myriad digitized operations of our single global computer. In the economy of abundance, we will inevitably go to the "pay-per-bit" and the "definition-on-demand" formulas, with instant debit at the source, at the time of use, simply because currency and current will become the same thing. As Mark Poster put it "The word 'money' now refers to a configuration of oxides on a tape stored in the computer department of a bank."[42]

In the computer, language meets with light, one tapping the other directly: absolute energy meeting absolute complexity. Lasers, fibre optics and electromagnetic fields are the new building blocks of intelligence. Ultra-fast processors will join high-speed integration in standards that will soon become uniform. That is the stuff of reality itself. The big reversal of our civilization is occurring right now, that is, between the conscious and unconscious realms. Not long ago, the world was dumb and we were clever. But the computer-assisted world is becoming very clever and faster than we are. Very soon our collective technological intelligence will outperform the individual organic ones both in speed and integration. It will be interesting to know how this unified cognitive organization will take care of the environment and poverty, and what criteria it will dictate for genetic engineering. For the time being, relax. We are not there yet.

CHAPTER SIX

THE STRESS OF SPEED

ACCELERATION AND CRISIS

"The appearance of a crisis can be read as not simply noise in the system but as the signal of emergence to the next level of historical order."[43]

– William Irwin Thompson

ACCELERATION, CRISIS AND INTEGRATION

THE EFFECTS of mass, speed and depth have always been with us. Print, telegraphy, photography, telephone, radio, cinema and television have each in turn accelerated the pace of a previous culture. Computers are specifically associated with speed; microchips have invaded and increased the speed of other technologies. Computers accelerate and disintegrate traditional cultural patterns, only to re-integrate them later in a new way.

ACCELERATION

Since the introduction of provincial lotteries, many Canadians have become overnight multimillionaires. However, this apparently desirable cause does not always carry desirable effect. Researchers and social workers remark upon the alarming number of people whose lives have been ruined by the sudden windfall. Stories abound of family rifts, divorces, sibling and neighbourhood rivalries, reckless spending and disastrous investment—events that have led to alcoholism, drugs, depression and, even, suicide. It would be a cliché to say that money, after all, does not bring happiness. It would be more accurate to say that such mishaps are the effect of a sudden acceleration. People who have never owned or managed large amounts of money before can be blown apart by the sheer energy it carries.

DESIGN, MATERIAL, SCALE AND PACE

If you submit any structure, physical or psychological, to a sudden acceleration, it can disintegrate. The resistance of a structure to stress is a function of its overall *design*, its *material*, its *scale* and, above all, its *pace*. These are important criteria to consider when providing for the health of organizations in times of rapid change. Whether a building, a bureaucracy or a mindset, all structures have certain proportions and they move or operate at a given speed.* Loss of scale or pace may translate into, say, workers losing their bearings. For example, the onslaught of mass culture via TV generated huge economies of scale for chain and department stores, that all but wiped out the small grocer and the local store. This was a painful loss of scale not only for the retailers but also for many customers, who felt de-personalized in the new megastores. Following acceleration, a reverse trend of integration can now be observed in shopping malls, which bring back the scale of the earlier, neighbourhood stores.

Instances of acceleration, sudden growth or intensification can

---

* In the case of building, the speed is zero. A building that is hit by a missile will break because it cannot yield at all. One the other hand, some buildings, such as bunkers, are better designed, with stronger material than others, to withstand the impact of missiles.

affect one or all of the features of a design. They can shatter or transform the whole structure. Besides altering its basic operating rhythm, one effect of acceleration is to sever the connections between the various parts of an organization, thereby dismantling it in time and space.

As a student, I had a summer job selling advertising space in a catalogue for African and Asian businesses. Its British-based publisher, now defunct, was used to working at an even, if not snail's, pace. Early on in this career, I realized that certain improvements in efficiency would yield ten times the amount of business raised by summer jobbers like myself. And having already quadrupled the income generated the year before, I presented a business plan involving little or no further investment of my time. To my amazement, none of my suggestions were taken up. Much later, I learned that my plans and initiatives were seen as having no purpose other than to rush things unnecessarily. Obviously, it had been a mistake to assume that this company was in the business of making money. That was rash. What I should have concluded is that business, especially a small English business, is an organic structure with its own rhythms and pace, and that any acceleration could threaten not only its stability, but also its raison d'être.

Depending upon the flexibility of the structure under observation, the consequence of acceleration may be disintegration or mutation. The acceleration of water molecules by heat turns the original substance into vapour. The acceleration of a local post office by a fax machine can result in loss of morale and even strikes. Similarly, business organizations, markets and even whole economies subjected to acceleration will either transform or expand to the breaking point. Inflation is an example of an economy boiling to vapour.

"INFLATION IS MONEY HAVING AN IDENTITY CRISIS"
– Marshall McLuhan

McLuhan's jest is more to the point. First, it reminds us that the message of inflation is not rising wages and prices, but the devaluation of currency in real terms. Second, it implies that inflation characterizes critical stages of economic history, when either the material support or the physical identity of money undergoes change. As money becomes lighter and lighter, offering less and less resistance to the speed of transactions, its meaning shifts from the material to the symbolic. As Tom Forester puts it, "when someone writes a cheque, no money changes hands . . . money is really *information* about money."[44]

Moving from its original hardware to its present software base, the value of money has ceased to be identified with its absolute material reference—a quantity of metal in hand, in the bank or at the bullion vault. It is now identified as a relative convention. Indeed, to be effective, pricing must not only be closely related to offer and demand, but also be commensurate with the proportions of the economy in which the pricing occurs. Thus: the price is a figure dependent upon a much larger ground and any change to the ground affects the relative value of the figure. The ground of western economies has shifted very often: *materially*, from the agricultural to the informational staple; in terms of *pace*, from heavy to light money; in terms of *scale*, it has shifted from local to global; and, overall, in terms of *design*, from nomadic to ecological. In today's increasingly globalized economy, which prevents individual nations from printing money without restraint, world trade balances become the criteria. Hence, local deficits begin to loom larger and larger and something must be done to hold them in check.

The conventional value of money is monitored daily, if not hourly. All the vagaries of local and global economies, their currencies and their interaction, are crunched together. This is an extremely labile situation that necessitates a symbolic rather than a material expression of value—an area of least resistance to accommodate market fluctuations. As McLuhan wrote, "all currencies, as electric information, are equally abstract and baseless; all spending becomes deficit spending, and the only practical form of taxation is inflation (taxation without representation)." The market is up in the airwaves and has been since computers took charge of playing with our money. Floating decimals and thin rippling fluctuations play at the interface of foreign exchange. Currencies are gently rubbing against one another and, at the edge where they meet, a fine shower of gold falls upon the money changers.

Strangely enough, your cash banknote is now behaving like a moderately fluctuating stock share, not like the once reliable symbol of your national economic system. If yesterday paper money was "the poor man's credit card," today it has become his stock and bond.

ELECTRONIC SPIN

Electronic Fund Transfers (EFT) allow for some rather clever though absurd financial operations. Some brokers specialize in investing huge sums of money for 48 hours or less. Let's say that a sum of money is on its way to pay for a merger or takeover bid. Ten million dollars invested at 10 percent for two days brings in about $5,500. The principal sum in full electronic flight doesn't seem to have to land anywhere. In this particular case, or in any stock exchange transactions, there seems to be no necessity for huge money transfers to be related to actual production. We can only assume that money's symbolic value must be expressed somewhere in a form that benefits the economy.

Investments can no longer be guaranteed by a material reality any more than your hard cash by some metal equivalent. Money, as information, is only guaranteed by more information about other information. The bulk of financial transactions are shifting from hardware to software, a situation that puts a spin on the rim of the economy and sends it swirling in a whirlpool of electrons. When money moves at the speed of light, value shifts from space and matter to time and design, even as the economy moves its centre of gravity from production to information and from goods to services. It seems possible for an inflationary trend to appear as the only supple variable among fiercely controlled parameters. Inflation absorbs the effect of disconnection between investment and production. Inflation is the self-adjusting buffer zone that absorbs and regulates value.

Left to its own devices, unchecked and misunderstood, inflation is no more than "taxation without representation." But perceived as the aura of an active, techno-cultural field, inflation is the process by which money and value recover their identity. As we shall see, a surgical inflationary move can actually prevent catastrophe.

CRISIS: FROM THE "BIG BANG" TO "BLACK MONDAY"

Two important dates herald the changes from the industrial mindset to techno-culturally driven financial wizardry: 1971, the year floating exchange rates were introduced, and October 27, 1986, when fixed commissions were ended by London's Stock Exchange. The latter is commonly known as the "Big Bang" of the new financial universe. Both deregulating decisions responded to acceleration brought about by computerization. Both ushered in eras of rapid fluctuations following times of rigid controls. Interestingly, on almost the same day, one year after the Big Bang, came Black Monday. It was our first serious brush with the inflation of increasingly electrified and accelerated investment decisions. Paradoxically, Adam Smith's law of the "invisible hand" of the self-regulating economy actually worked to restore a lost equilibrium in that hugely volatile environment.

"Black Monday" was the computer-assisted stock exchange crash of October 19, 1987. Millions of shares were sold in a few hours, bringing the New York Stock Exchange Index down to a full third of its highest level. Some economists blamed the crash on the investment system's unmanageable complexity and lack of safeguards. On one hand, individual investors and traders were responsible for conscious investment decisions. On the other, the accumulation and acceleration of such decisions, interpreted by the stock exchange's expert systems, tipped the balance between human and machine control. Mechanization took command with unpredictable consequences.

But why did this crash not follow the model of 1929, which ushered in ten years of Depression and caused a rash of suicides? Because the first was an industrial crash, befalling industrial mindsets, while the other was a self-adjusting epileptic seizure of a techno-cultural field recovering its own equilibrium.

CRISIS MANAGEMENT

As I've suggested, the new breed of investors had been playing with information and turning it into money, another kind of information. However, the Federal Reserve Bank knew that once the gap between investment and production became too large, the situation would result in crisis. Now that it had happened, on Black Monday, what was to be done? The answer, paradoxically, was to invest more money—that is, more information—in the system. Even at the risk of losing the money immediately. This would shore up the value made from information with more information. And in this way, the market would quickly regain its composure. There was, of course, no cause for alarm once investors' risks were covered by the government's risk, that is, by the whole economy putting itself on the line. That attitude, however, is bound to generate a series of other fruitful crises, which may eventually teach us a thing or two about the shortcomings of representational money as a medium for social development.

Crisis is the moment of change, of metamorphosis: we can imagine that a caterpillar is in deep crisis at the moment it turns into a butterfly. We all think that the word crisis means something terrible, but it doesn't. It means something clever, peaceful and good. Crisis comes from the ancient Greek word *krino*, which means 'to evaluate, judge or decide.' A crisis is a time for judgement and an object of judgement. Though many crises are occasioned by truly unpredictable occurrences, many more arise from the breakdown of old systems as they are overtaken by the new. The Bhopal disaster might have been predicted—if not averted—by tracking the safety records of the local management. But a real breakthrough was the sudden discovery of the new context of public accountability provided by electronic communications. We have all become our brother's keepers in the world of instant communications. Facing a crisis, many people waste their time watching the old order go down, deploring their fate and regretting the world that has gone by. But it takes critical judgement in critical times to understand that the real story is what's coming. Then the task of deciding is easy, and fascinating.

BREAKDOWN

Ever since Watergate, breakdowns are becoming increasingly visible, moral lapses in high places increasingly uncomfortable. Why is that? Are we about to become sensitive? Precisely: we are becoming more aware and more informed. Electricity is lighting up hidden recesses everywhere. There is reason to suppose that even the minimal video and computer facilities of eastern Europe helped to expose the inequities of totalitarian power. Living in the information environment means at least two things. First, we are all becoming beacons of information. Second, so much can be known, and made known, that there is nowhere to hide.[45]

The wars of the last 100 years can be interpreted as crises that have served to destroy one world order so as to replace it with another. Even the so-called Cold War was effectively a new world order. Although the nuclear threat has prevented all-out frontal wars and turned aggressors into guerrillas or terrorists, it has educated all cultures to the invisible unity of the planet itself. The moment the threat was lifted by changes in East–West relations, a conventional war was waged in the Persian Gulf. War can be the result of the acceleration of a slow culture by a faster culture. The recent example of the Gulf War makes that obvious, but war is a very painful way to get an education. One can look at war as a breakdown, and piously deplore it or see the breakthrough behind it. The Gulf Crisis was an example of breakdown as crackdown, not breakthrough. In major breakdowns, a quick mind appreciates two things: one, that such a situation won't happen again in quite the same way, and two, that the time has arrived for a new understanding of how these things happen. Here is what William Irwin Thompson wrote in December 1983, commenting upon whether McLuhan or Orwell had a better understanding of world events in 1984.

> One sure indication that nation-states are about to be integrated in another level of historical order can be seen in the cumulative nature of global conflicts today. Tribe fights tribe in Africa and Northern Ireland; a people fights another people in the middle East and nation-state fights nation-state everywhere: from the sacking of Spanish and Italian trucks by French farmers to the destruction of Syrian missiles by American or Israeli jets. Precisely because global forms of communication have integrated everyone in a planetary culture. The traditional forms of identity are threatened and are fighting for survival with the hysteria of the terrorist, but as these struggles are immediately played back to the world through the global means of communication that the terrorist exploits, this negative use of television only serves to energize the global integration of all peoples in a new world culture.[46]

A few years on, the situation has already changed dramatically, in spite of some players still playing roughly the same game. Globalization has now moved from the background to the forefront of people's consciousnesses.

FROM CHERNOBYL TO THE BERLIN WALL. BREAKDOWN AS BREAKTHROUGH

In the Chernobyl breakdown, people began to see that nuclear technology involves taking large and unnecessary risks. The Soviets had emulated the Americans with their own version of the Three Mile Island disaster. But they lost face to the West because of the bad press about world-wide nuclear pollution. Was this the inspiration to pull out their intermediate nuclear forces from the European front? One incident may have nothing to do with the other. Then again, in the larger context, Gorbachev may have found in Chernobyl the need to rewrite the rules of the East–West game and to adapt to the new conditions of media image play. At the time the Berlin Wall went up, McLuhan had already suggested that it would never withstand the pressure applied by the faster western culture upon the slower eastern one. By refusing to send the Soviet Army to put down protests against Honecker, Gorbachev showed the qualities of a statesman in crisis management. The breakdown of the Wall translated into the biggest breakthrough in East–West relations since the end of the Second World War.

People often think that crises happen in a kind of fog, where you can't make head or tail of the situation. But more often than not, the crisis itself reveals the pattern. There is a fine account of breakdown leading to breakthrough in Edgar Allen Poe's "Descent into the Maelstrom." A sailor and his brother are in a boat in a huge whirlpool. While the brother hangs on to the ship's mast in terror, the sailor observes how the big boats and barges caught in the swirling foam would go down to crash on the bottom, as if dragged there by their own weight, whereas lighter structures rose, benefiting from an upward counter-current. Taking a momentous decision, and having tried in vain to persuade his brother to let go of the mast, the sailor grabs a barrel thrown alongside and jumps in. He is carried to safety on the outer rim of the spin, only to see his own brother go down with the crashing boat.

BREAKTHROUGH COMES FROM STUDYING THE PATTERN OF THE BREAKDOWN

Recessions in the seventies redirected government spending from underwriting consumerism in the sixties to supporting the present interplay of deficit economies. One interesting response to crisis has been the invention of equity debt-refinancing, which happened when Brazil refused to honour interest payments on its national debt. This involves buying into the debt to leverage tax concessions, rebates and privileges in order to build equity in local industries. This is a real breakthrough, since it combines good business sense— protecting an otherwise lost investment—with adroit aid to developing countries.

Crisis management is especially valuable in times of transition. The transition today is from what was once called the "history of the western world" into "the history of the Earth." With communications travelling at the speed of thought, strictly local economies make no more sense than strictly local ecologies. At every second, we are bound to one another by global events as surely as the weather. Our businesses and their crises fit very well in this scenario—all the better when executives understand where they stand in the large scheme, the larger context. There will always be time to work back to the specifics of a predicament, whether it concerns international telecommunication standards or employee resistance to computerization. Like any major corporation, but with the complication of high visibility, governments often take the blame for patterns of mismanagement. Next time around, perhaps governments should explain on TV how they are working to maintain public confidence without threatening the system. To do this properly, they'll need to understand how to inspire authority, precision, compassion and calmness among the media.

The only sure thing that we have learned so far is the "the future isn't what it used to be." The next stage is to recognize that we are primitives in a new, global culture. To grow from the status of mere victims of our crises to that of explorers, we must develop a sense of critical judgment in critical times.

CHAPTER SEVEN

BABEL AND JERICHO

ARCHITECTURAL METAPHORS
FOR TECHNOLOGICAL
AND PSYCHOLOGICAL
CATASTROPHIES

And the Lord came down to see the city and the tower, which the children of men builded. And the Lord said, behold, the people are one, and they have all one language; and this they begin to do; and now nothing will be restrained from them, which they have imagined to do. Go to, let us go down, and there confound their language, that they may not understand one another's speech.

(Genesis 11:5–7)

N THIS PASSAGE the oldest book of the Bible acknowledges the limitless, godlike power of language; the first software to create, shape and command matter. It is because they are endowed with language that nothing, except the confusion of languages, can stop the "children of men." Babel and Jericho were both software catastrophes, the first was tragic and the other comic. The breakdown of communications in Babel addressed a classic—almost Greek—case of hubris: the architects of Babel were punished by the very thing that gave them pride, the universal quality of their language.

But the fall of Jericho proposed an alternative: "And it shall come to pass, that when they make a long blast with the ram's horn, and when ye hear the sound of the trumpet, all the people shall shout with a great shout; and the wall of the city shall fall down flat, and the people shall ascend up every man straight before him" (Joshua 6:5). The combination of three kinds of sound was necessary to bring the walls down: the blast from the ram's horn, the sound of the trumpets and the people's great shout. Whatever you make of the prescription, it points to a belief in the ability of sound to pulverize the hardest obstacle. As a victory of software over hardware, Jericho symbolizes a revolution in physics, a paradigmatic transformation. Today our world is poised between two options, the Babelian disintegration and the Jericho metamorphosis.

Philippe Quéau puts the problem of the modern world squarely into the Babelian purview by suggesting that the issue in Babel was not that the architects did not understand each other, but that they understood each other only too well.[47] It is the same universalism in today's trends in compatibility and standardization in information-processing software that beg comparison with the perils of the accumulated power of a universal language. In spite of much social unrest and a world-wide recession, our relentless technological acceleration may give us the impression that everything is going too well, that we are going too fast towards a destiny that we cannot clearly distinguish, as if we were collectively experiencing the rush of a consensual hallucination. We sense the imminence of a catastrophe not necessarily in Biblical terms but rather in terms of French philosopher René Thom's description of a phenomenon that, under the accumulation of its own weight and speed, suddenly reaches a point of reversal.

Sudden technological and social acceleration without preparation can indeed lead to disintegration, as both World Wars have amply demonstrated. This surely is the Babel side. However, we are beginning to become accustomed to speed. Our computers are accelerating our psychological responses and our reaction time much faster than planes, trains and automobiles ever did. Computers are also combining, unifying and synchronizing the activities of the global electronic network. We are beginning to perceive this unity as consisting of huge waveforms of electrical currents in electromagnetic fields. This is the soundwave that could bring down all the walls of cities and nation-states. The reversal we should expect is not a disaster but a transformation—a radically new image of humankind.

The western cultural and technological heritage comes from a single source: phonological literacy. Hebrews, Greeks and Romans were "People of the Book." While the Old and the New Testaments have provided the backbone and the guidelines of occidental culture over the last three millennia, the West's principal and dominant information-processing system (until the appearance of electricity) has been the alphabet. The alphabet has been the fundamental programming device of the Western cultures. It is from the alphabet that the West has derived its characteristic techno-centric drive. The alphabet behaved as a cultural accelerator, taking full advantage of the articulation of language to translate thought into technologies. The technological temptation, ever-present in the Hebraic tradition, probably comes from the mastery over language that their high-performance orthography gave the ancient Hebrews.

However, the Hebrews' fear of the consequences of their own innovations also came from the consonantal nature of their particular brand of alphabet. Because vowels are not represented in the writings of Semitic scripts, the text is never completely independent of the context. Not only is it impossible to read Hebrew without knowing the language itself, it is also quite difficult to read it without a fairly extensive knowledge of the context of the statements. Hence, it is necessary for most if not all Hebrew texts to refer to a common ground, a shared knowledge base that does not allow for many ideational breakaways. Knowledge is sacred in that sense and cannot be tampered with. However, within the constraints of a deeply religious mindset, phonological writing is, of necessity, subversive because it objectifies thinking in verbal, not iconic terms. To see your thoughts written down allows you to work on them, to refine them, to come back to them and to modify them. The expansion of thinking by the phonological representation complexifies and accelerates thinking. It invites verbal and linguistic explorations or "essays." The temptation to innovate, to think on our own, already latent in Eve's desire to taste the fruit of knowledge, must be great indeed. But it may have been quite difficult for the ancient Hebrew reader to experience without guilt the freedom of pure mindplay, of innovation for innovation's sake. In the Hebrew tradition, it is not only sinful to succumb to temptation, but even merely to think about it.

By comparison, anybody can read anything written in Roman alphabets whatever the language being represented. By allowing the reading of the text to be fairly independent of knowledge about the context, roman alphabets allow texts to be entirely decontextualized from their sources. There is no real need or urgency for the Romanized reader to refer the text to an all-encompassing context, no reason to feel guilty for dreaming up alternatives to the common lore. Fiction, theory and scientific experimentation were given full reign in endless combinations, recombinations and permutations of linguistic strings in literate forms. To this day, we owe our free-thinking habits and our unrepentant technological drive to early alphabetization in school. It is also in this non-Hebraic perspective that our relationship to technological innovation ought to be considered and that the threat of a new Babelian catastrophe ought to be reassessed.

Genesis 11 does not specify how the Lord confounded language to disperse the people. He could have used writing. The hidden historical ground of the Babel myth may be that Semitic literacy, taking over from Egyptian pictographic orthographies, emphasized the phonological over the ideographic representations of languages, thus emphasizing differences in local dialects and specialized uses of the common language. This hypothesis is all the more probable when one compares the explosive consequences of alphabetic literacy with the power of ideograms to maintain stability in Egypt and China over millennia in spite of vast local disparities in dialects and languages.

The alphabet was a powder keg. Among the many consequences of the literate fragmentation, exemplified typically by the invention of the printing press in the Renaissance, were several explosions; that of Latin as the lingua franca into the vernacular languages, that of the Holy Roman Empire into nation and city-states and that of the medieval religious unity into Reform and Protestantism. These various explosions generated vicious and protracted wars, but perhaps, the most consistent effect of the literate revolution in the West was the systematic levelling of vertical structures into horizontal ones. Soon after the alphabet began to take hold of the ruling and especially the merchant classes, there was a gradual shift from vertical-feudal hierarchies (God-given power) to horizontal democracies. Few signs are more telling than the profound architectural changes from the High Middle Ages to the late Renaissance. A kind of "horizontal imperative" changed the orientation of building as well as of thinking. The thinking moved from an up-down God-to-Man relationship, to an exclusively earth-bound conception exemplified by Voltaire's famous *"Il faut cultiver notre jardin."* As for architecture, while the cathedral of Cologne can stand as a perfect example of pre-catastrophic Babelian verticality, built over several centuries by the common faith of people who spoke a common language, the buildings of the following era adopted the horizontality of the written line and the faithful symmetry of the two pages of an open book.

Paradoxically, with all its explosive potential, the invention of the Greek alphabet was also a kind of revenge of humankind against Babelian dispersion. It quickly became the standard writing system for all Indo-European languages except Russian and associated Slavic tongues. It was the first "common carrier" of information in the West. Even as the alphabet provided a powerful impetus to highlight local and vernacular languages, hence emphasizing local identities and local cultures in the various linguistic communities of Europe, it also provided a common ground for international trade, association and technology transfer. At the cognitive level, alphabetic literacy became the common source of all the sensory references of sense-making in the elaboration of meaning. Literate people have a tendency to translate their sensory experience into words and their sensory responses into verbal structures. This comes from their habit of translating strings of printed letters into sensory images in order to make sense of what they read.

Today, the new "common sense" is the digital process. Via digitization, all sources of information, including material phenomena and natural processes, including our sensory simulations—for example in virtual reality systems—are homogenized into strings of 0/1 sequences. Part of the "Jericho effect" comes from the ability of an electric code to infiltrate all substances and translate them into itself. Electricity takes off from the alphabet. This is why we are experiencing both the thrill and the anxiety of acceleration once more.

THE NEW ARCHITECTS

The new architecture is within and outside of the computer; it is made of cable, fibre-optics and hertzian and satellite-supported communication networks. It structures the operability of programs and databases. It structures the functioning of State and Economy. All these systems and networks are tributaries of one single, overarching technology: electricity. Electricity is the new single, common language. It is by nature cohesive and implosive, not explosive like the alphabet. To be useful and increase their market value, innovative communication technologies such as data networks, videotext and videoconferencing systems require maximum interoperability and common standards. In spite of the tendency of systems producers and developers to develop proprietary standards, a knee-jerk economic reflex inherited from our Babelian Mechanical Age, the trend is towards integration and the market itself will eventually wipe out all the players who refuse to play ball. Computers gave us power over the screen and allowed us to personalize information-processing. It is not the world that is becoming global; we are.

That's the good news. The bad news is that every technological innovation brings about an opposite counter-reaction: globalization encourages hyperlocalization, which in many parts of the world, brings social unrest, various patterns of racism and armed conflicts. That is the double-edged Babelian paradox that is present in the redefinition of local identities and allegiances. To the extent that people are globalized, they will also emphasize their local identity all the more. The threat of Babel revisited lurks in the Gulf War, Somalia and the former Yugoslavia.

However, the haunting memory of Babel in the collective unconscious does not necessarily percolate from current issues of political and ethnic strife. We have gone through much more violent and generalized strife without talking about Babel. A Babelian fear may arise from the deeper implications of our new-found power over matter and life, with its social, political, psychological and religious consequences. The New Architects are the nuclear power engineers, the molecular engineers, the genetic engineers. The new Tower is a double helix and the new Babelian dream is the Genome project (the transcription of the entire human genetic code) that, with the best intentions in the world, is about to give genetic engineering the unprecedented power of social control.

Our genetic code is the next level of our universal languages. It should soon become apparent that a certain loss of balance between the powers of nature and those of culture was built into the phonetic alphabet. The image of the alphabet still resides in our scientific interpretation of the relationships between DNA and RNA. Recombinant genetic engineering allows strings of genetic instructions to be decontextualized from their source and transplanted into another, different cell, originating from a different individual and, even, from a different species altogether.

The fact that we are indeed embarking on a course of total control over nature is abundantly demonstrated by our recent predilection for the vocabulary of artificial reality. Words such as "virtual" reality, "cyber" space, "real" time, "artificial" life, and "endo-" and "nanotechnologies," are enjoying a vertical growth curve. They are clear linguistic symptoms of a "cyborg" trend that seeks to blend organic and technical realms. To say nothing about the uncertain and uneasy relationship that ever more invasive technologies enjoy with our bodies, the more pressing issue for the New Architects is that this biotechnical realm constitutes a desirable technological support for human destinies. There is absolutely no assurance that the experts have the right context, or indeed, any context at all, to base their research options on. And the fact that medical and pharmaceutical interest groups are already bidding for licensing control over the Genome project's first ascertained discoveries is not destined to reassure anyone. After decades of being hostages to the industrial-military complex, we are threatened with a new kind of seizure of the body politic, that of the industrial-medical complex.

While scientists and technocrats are busy looking to perfect our bodies and our minds according to the old model of the renaissance man, our daily technologies are changing us insidiously in a manner that will soon be unrecognizable to obsolete scientific paradigms. The scientific image of the human is that of a perfect machine with replaceable parts. In genetic engineering, the image is only slightly improved. The machine can build itself according to specifications only if you know how to modify the programming. The future of health and fitness lies in the concept embodied by the replicant in *Bladerunner*. The vicious circle is easy to predict: techno-science will build scientifically balanced organisms to perform scientifically calculated operations to perfection. The computer made flesh. There is no soul to this machine because there is no room for anything but an operational self in the scientific/robotic vision of this being. We certainly need a Babelian catastrophe to avoid that destiny, if it is indeed the direction we are going.

But, in fact, it isn't. Science is no better than science fiction at predicting reality. Scientists, for example, have no idea about the deeper and largely unconscious implications of America's new "political correctness" movement. As a reaction to the threat of an overwhelming control of nature by culture, the tendency called political correctness (PC), which has taken hold in North America like a forest fire and is spreading less easily in Europe, may be an unconscious grassroot response to the fear created by scientific and technological control of what constitutes the best image of humankind. Whatever one can object to in the sometimes oppressive attitudes of PC activists, the notion that each member of society, irrespective of race, colour, religion, gender, state of health, level of education, condition of fortune and class, personal attributes or lack thereof is entitled to equal status in the social setting is worth exploring. It may save us from Babel.

ART TO THE RESCUE: "SEE MORE, HEAR MORE AND FEEL MORE"

Science does not know where we are going because it has abandoned the quest for "why" to devalued religions. It cannot know the future because it is hardly capable of assessing the present. Lost in conceptual spinnings, interlocking theories and stupefyingly simplistic experiments, most professional scientists are clearly void of any but the crudest perceptions. As Karl-Heinz Stockhausen suggested, today we are invited to "see more, hear more and feel more." This is an artist's statement. Few people apart from artists are capable of predicting the present. Our technologies already make us see more, hear more and feel more. But no self-respecting psychologist in any American university would even be willing to consider that the extensions of our sensory experiences might have a feedback effect on our psychological experience. The role of the artist today, as always, is to recover for the general public the larger context that has been lost by science's exclusive investigations of text.

But Stockhausen's suggestion is not that we be satisfied with television carrying our eyes to the end of the planet, or that we marvel that the telephone brings us voices from afar, or that we learn to touch screens and virtual textures. What he recommends is that we let our senses teach us to become new people, better adjusted to the real dimensions of mankind extended beyond the reach of our natural senses. The job of the artist who addresses the new media and the new machines is to not to praise or condemn technology, but to bridge the gap between technology and psychology. Our new technological artforms in John Sanborn's videos, in Karl Sims' computer graphics, in Dieter Jung's holography, in Monica Fleishmann's virtual realities are but expanded metaphors of our technically extended senses. And a word such as "telesensitivity" only begins to describe it.

To see more is not merely to see further away, beyond the confines of our walls and our present horizons. It is to develop a new precision and flexibility in our eyes; it is to see behind our backs, as well as in front of our eyes; it is to perceive the world not exclusively in a frontal relationship, but in a total surround; it is to multiply the facets of our eyes and the objects of our simultaneous gaze as if all the cameras of the world were the realization of a new Argus.

To hear more is to know how to find the sound behind the sound, behind the fury of the city and behind the cacophony of the media. To hear more is to learn with David Hykes and the Harmonic Choir that, yes, for centuries we have obliterated the harmonics of those sounds that support meaning, the only ones we know how to hear. For centuries we have failed to hear the divine subtleties of echoing and blending harmonies ever present in the environment. John Cage said that silence is the sum of all the sounds of the environment at once. He could also have said that silence is alive.

To feel more is the most important. Paracelsus said that the ear is not an extension of the skin, but that the skin is truly an extension of the ear. Of course, after we learn to read and write, we learn to close within our skin the silent contents of our minds. We learn to use our skin as an excluding device. We become quite terrified of touch, of bodily contact, of other people's bodies and of our own, more than of anybody else's. Then the skin can only hurt. It needs the protection of layers of clothing. Other people's touch can only hurt. Our privacy needs the protection of guilt.

To the electronic extension of our body, such a perception of the skin is abhorrent. McLuhan suggested that "in the electric age, we wear all mankind as our skin." That makes perfect sense. The skin as a communicating, not a protecting device makes perfect sense. Eugene Gendlin, the little-heeded American psychologist who invented the notion of "felt-meaning" to describe how our bodies process information with as much, if not more speed and accuracy than our minds, opened for us a new field of tactile perceptions, beyond the limits of the individual body. I cannot watch too much violence on TV, not because I fear that it will desensitize me as so many unimaginative commentators hasten to suggest, but because I cannot take too many blows in my neuromuscular responses.

The violence of the few is the result of the insensitivity of the many. To feel more is to begin to get ready for a proper understanding of the world we are getting into. It is a way to avoid a Babelian catastrophe. To expand the reach of our sociopsychological responsibility, as well as to discover a new global and collective Renaissance, the role of art is paramount. The real issue is to change our perceptions, not just our theories. Telecommunication art helps us to perceive that we are becoming larger people as we look back on our planet from space and discover that the real size of our collective body is the planet itself. Interactive arts and the proliferation of sensory interfaces can make us realize that we use our extended minds and bodies as tuning mechanisms to monitor the state of health of the Earth. We are invited to refine our proprioception to extend our point of being (rather than our point of view) from wherever we are to wherever our technically extended senses can allow us to reach.

CHAPTER EIGHT

CYBERDESIGN

DESIGN CRITERIA FOR CYBERACTIVITY

VIRTUAL REALITY

A T THE HEAD MOUNTED DISPLAY (HMD) unit of the University of North Carolina at Chapel Hill, there is a VR system that allows a designer to select basic 3-D shapes (spheres, cubes and pyramidal structures) and expand them to desired sizes, combine them, work them over with various techniques of edging and proportioning, all in real time. The designer can see the concept grow into shape and walk in or around it immediately. Virtual reality allows you to physically enter the products of your own imagination.

VR is as close to "pure" design as one can get in applied technology because it is entirely based on software activities. Apart from the computer workstation, a pair of "eyephones" and a Dataglove, there is nothing material about it until a command is sent to get something done or built. The systems in existence consist of various types of interfaces connecting users to full-surround graphic and sound environments provided by a computer. To enter virtual reality you can either wear Eyephones that present you with stereoscopic 3-dimensional vistas of a graphic world, or project your image into that world without actually enclosing yourself in it. To operate in the projected world, you wear a glove, called Dataglove, that allows you to move in the graphic universe and handle objects in it.

VR has been in the hands of a special breed of artist-engineers from the very beginning. The original VR interface is the HMD unit that was first developed at MIT and the University of Utah during the late sixties and early seventies by computer scientist Ivan Sutherland. However, as Howard Rheingold[48] rightly points out, the idea of getting the watcher into the picture came first to cinematographer Morton Heilig and the realization of the first full-surround multi-sensory machine was his Sensorama (1960), which is kept under cover in his backyard and still works after over thirty years. The Sensorama is an apparatus that allows a user to experience a film in 3-D, by touch (according to approximately the same principle as was adopted for more recent "sensurround" movies), smell and, of course, auditory stimulations. Another artist-engineer whose concept of VR differed by projecting the user's image into the virtual world is Myron Krueger. Krueger spent years developing his Video-place environment where the image of the user projected onto the screen creates elegant graphic and sound events. Krueger has only been achieving international recognition as a VR pioneer recently.

It does indeed take a special kind of sensibility to foresee the potential of VR. Heilig never succeeded in finding enough backing to develop what could have been the first VR system. VR was subsequently developed by an institution not known to have been short of money, the U.S. Department of Defense. The HMD was adapted for military flight simulation by people whose practical motivation was to replace costly and potentially fatal training on military aircraft by simulated computerized piloting. Most work on flight simulation consisted—and still consists—in improving the visual, auditory and tactile simulations of landing and take-off, tracking, bombing and air-to-air combat situations.

At the other end of the design spectrum are the many artists, such as Krueger, but also Thomas Zimmerman, Jaron Lanier, Graham Smith, David Rokeby and others who have recognized in VR the best experimental ground for the technological exploration of the human sensorium. The relationship of VR to art is predicated on its potential for sensory expression. There is a whole new field for artists to discover sensory patterns, technically extended sensory projections and their interaction with users. Designers will probably want to pay attention to what artists are doing in this field because soon that is where their best ideas may come from. Today some of the most interesting work in VR is what seems to sprout spontaneously from the artist's studio. Indeed, the inspiration for VR artwork wells from the unfettered probing of the biological ground of our psychological responses.

From a practical point of view, VR is to the drawing table what video recording and instant playback are to celluloid filming. Its responses happen in real time. VR can potentially reduce, if not eliminate altogether, the time and space interval between intention and realization. Eventually VR will go the way of word-processing and desk-top publishing that allows the writer the total flexibility of instant and yet erasable publication and distribution. Thus VR is almost a direct technological extension and expression of the mental processes involved in designing. Mental visions are given graphic shapes that can respond at will to changes, almost as things happen in one's own mind. You can work in VR with the added benefit of being able to actually enter the contents of your extended mind and even to share the product of your thought unambiguously with co-workers. VR will eventually allow people to meet and work together in virtual stations that already bear the name of "virtual common."

If there ever was a definite, teleological rather than serendipitous, direction to the development of electronic technologies, VR could well represent its present synthesis. It seems to be the logical outcome and the point of convergence of many other electronic technologies. Behind VR developments there are strong market-potential driven stimuli. For example, at the technical level, VR seems to be ready to take full advantage of the trend to convert analog to digital signals in High Definition Television. VR combines the "live" directness of video technologies with the flexibility of computer intervention. To improve distribution and collaborative use, as well as rendering techniques, VR is pushing rapid developments in signal compression and transmission. Along with improved communication networks and electronic "highways," it can support both broadcast and special services. Coupled with neural network technologies VR can push automation to autonomation, that is, granting controlled levels of autonomy to automated electronic robots.

At a deeper level, VR research brings to convergence the most recent discoveries in psychological as well as technological software. Just as the quest for improved artificial intelligence (AI) and expert systems in computers drove brain research faster and further than if it had been left to the medical and academic institutions, VR is already inspiring an accelerated drive to understand the organic underpinnings and the sensory-laden complexities of human intelligence. Not surprisingly there is also an impetus for adding touch to our visual and auditory expertise in simulations, to make the experience more "real," more direct and ultimately more controllable. Thanks to digitization, it is possible to translate any set of inputs into different sets of outputs. Digitization has become the "common sense" of technology and psychology in computer software.

Once VR technology reaches the level of maturation predicted by actual trends, it is likely to change the levels and processes of any production into objects and products of design. VR will eventually penetrate media in news reporting and make people participate in events as it already does in entertainment. Children's education will be accelerated considerably by full-bodied contact with different types of experiences in knowledge and recreational fields. One day, museums will be jam-packed with VR reconstitutions of environments distant in time and space. Medical practice and research, and care for disabled and handicapped people will be facilitated by applied VR technologies. It is clear that VR industries will depend first and foremost on the quality and versatility of their designers.

The present state of VR technology is still fairly crude. The image definition is poor and the frame renewal rate is often too slow to give a "real-time" impression of the correlations between one's movements and the effects in the graphic simulations. But the progress of

VR is relentless and it will eventually take over the economy—just as television once did – because it stimulates the convergence of market pressures and growing psychological needs. VR is the first technology ever that has hit the popular imagination before it has even reached anything close to maturity. Even as a concept, VR is already powerful enough to help change the thinking of mainstream industry and rejuvenate our exhausted post-industrial economy. We need this new thinking to respond to the challenge of VR.

CYBERDESIGN

"Cyberdesign" is design reconsidered by virtual reality. It is an aspect of design about to move from the periphery to the centre of industrial attention. Cyberdesign is what design becomes when it is supported by cyberactive systems. Cyberdesign is a critical addition to the vocabulary of designers because it is about to become a major industry.

Design parameters are the features of design susceptible to change and interaction within cyberactive systems. The designer's task is to provide a choice of integrated parameters that will shape the response of the system. It takes a professional designer to second guess what is needed and what isn't, in ever more complex integrated self-adjusting environments of possibilities. If it is possible to open or close a wall of liquid crystal displays, as one can see in Dutch culturologist Kriet Titulaer's "house of the future," then it is also possible to change its colour or make it interactive with the people moving by. Such features are like elements of a puzzle that the user may sometime want to put together alone. The complexity of parameters to be controlled requires a level of "metadesign," that is, designing a system for use by the buyer/client . The designer's task is to provide a choice of integrated parameters that will shape the response of the system. An example of the complexities involved can be read in the history of word-processing systems that have seen software developers' fortunes rise and collapse over single features.

Cyberdesign could be understood as an offshoot of traditional design but applied specifically to that new figure in the market, the "prosumer."

Alvin Toffler coined that term to highlight the latest trends in marketing, which showed that many potential buyers were not content with being consumers anymore, but they wanted more and more to be in on the act of production.[49] James Joyce had foreseen this development long ago when he asked in jest: "My consumers, aren't they my producers?" What he meant, of course, was that the relationship between production and consumption is one of strong interdependence. What is happening today, however, as a result of the computerization of the social body, is that people want to help produce their own goods. It is not just a matter of "customizing" the product, to make it fit more tightly to the individual needs of the buyer. It is primarily an issue of *empowerment.*

As technology empowers people, consumers develop the need to exercise more control over their immediate environment. As we move towards a consumer-directed rather than producer-directed culture, industry will come to realize that designing features that reflect the power of the consumer will have to be built into the products. The prosumer generation was born during the eighties, the era of yuppies and of computer networks. Computers allowed people to talk back to their screens, to reclaim control of their mental life from television and to take an active part in the organization of their environment, both local and global.

Prosumerism is far from peaking, yet it has already introduced the need for personalized empowerment as a critical feature of many goods destined to mass consumption. To give a small but ubiquitous example, no self-respecting businessperson can be content with a basic telephone. Add-on functions such as automatic answering, call-waiting, call-forwarding, call-screening and remote message-collecting, etc. are all destined to give added confidence to the user that he or she has increased control over his or her life. Our TV sets themselves have become little production units to respond to the technical sophistication of video-recording and video-editing systems. New computer-assisted desktop publishing, editing, recording and multi-media operating systems land on our desks every two months.

Cyberdesign is the kind of design philosophy that addresses the sensibility of the prosumer. To the extent that sixties and seventies mass markets were predicated on planned obsolescence and packaging, that speed markets of the eighties were ruled by instant communications and high technology, the nineties economy will probably be based on inviting the consumer to take part in production decisions. The leaders will use cyberactive systems and they will inspire a changed approach in many other fields as well, for instance in education, entertainment, self-help services and perhaps even politics— witness the resurgence of populism (service-driven government) in North America.

From the empowerment imperative come other criteria for design that could prove fundamental with tomorrow's mass markets for goods and services. Empowerment translates into improved customizing, greater versatility of products to allow for more choices from a single technology. The inherent selectivity of the desktop industry will allow greater penetration of specialized niche markets. On the consumer side customers want "bells and whistles" with their TV sets, CD players and microwave ovens, not because they need them or actually plan to use them, but because such add-ons empower them. That they could use the features if they were needed is enough justification to spend more. When people buy these systems, they are not buying services, not even status; they are buying power.

Empowerment also brings out the sine qua non condition of *user-friendliness*. The learning process to use the technology should be built into the system and not required from the customer. There are several million people who would have remained computer-illiterate to this day, had it not been for the invention of Apple's Macintosh that you could learn to use in one afternoon. Compare that to the months of laborious practice the users of most IBM systems and their clones required before they finally caved in and adopted the Windows desktop environment. User-friendliness meets the requirements of instant gratification—a legacy from the consuming bulimia fed by the TV era—and of intuitive rather than inductive usage. Perhaps because we have been spoiled by so many different technological helpers, but also because we have lost the habit of making physical efforts, we feel that our machines ought to obey instantly, without asking from us anything but mere attention, and sometimes not even that.

That is why cyberactive systems operate best in real-time. But *real-timeliness* is not just another demand made by our thirst for instant gratification. Of course, the speed at which our orders are carried is a measure of our power, but the taste for real-timeliness comes from the new level of proximity and intimacy that technologies evoke within our bodies and our minds. Certainly, Walkman earphones, VR eyephones, datasuits and datagloves entertain an almost organic relationship with our physical being. We are getting used to conversing with our computer screens as if they were but extensions of our minds, carrying on interactive dialogues that also bear some of the marks of organicity. The consequence is that we are beginning to expect of our machines that they react to our commands with the same intuitive speed as our own limbs and senses.

We think of design primarily as a concern for our eyes; this is an effect of our immediate literate past. There has been some improvement in non-visually based design since we invented the concept of ergonomics, but computer-assisted design research is pushing the limits of sensory simulation and stimulation and it will add awareness of the subtleties of the other senses. Where, not long ago, we used to enter data into our machines or press a button to make them work, now we are beginning to put them on, like virtual bodies.

However, there is one last criterion that somehow seems to have evolved spontaneously, on its own, in the post-industrial culture— something that we might call *inconspicuousness*. Things want to hide, to meld into the background. Functions cease to be evident in some quality machines. This discretion is like a new world of "manners" in design. Although the trend of global economic austerity may account for a recent tendency to avoid external signs of wealth, there may be more to the developing aesthetics of disappearance than an economic base.

There is an inverse proportion between high-tech and visibility: that is, the more high-tech, the more discrete the medium; the lower the technology, the more bells and whistles are needed to prop it up. For example, compare the design of Sony ghettoblasters with the new design of Sony TVs, which have become almost intelligent stations instead of dumb terminals. Even the remote-control systems tend to minimalize all functions to the point of the absurd (I can never find where to adjust the picture for tone or herringbone interferences!).

However, what disappears to the eye, often resurfaces in touch: indeed, in keeping with the metaphor of the central nervous system, the continuity between organic and technological electricity is a matter best handled by feeling. Children who sharpen their hand-eye co-ordination with hand-held videogames experience touch in ways that rival the skills of the professional pianist! Designers will want to know the differences between the articulations of touch as contact and the articulations of touch as remote pressure. Electricity can simulate both to different effects, and industrial designers in Japan are well aware of interaction possibilities with simple commands activated by proximity alone.

Most of the design criteria invoked here are introduced and made relevant by the new technologies. None of user-friendliness, multi-sensoriality, real-timeliness or miniaturization were conceived of in the modernist or even the post-modernist eras. And yet, such criteria are not difficult to identify or to understand. They can be learned "on-the-job" so to speak. Other criteria may not as yet have surfaced and will be discovered as the true nature of cyberactive systems unfolds.

Still, there is also a deeper process at work. It seems as if every major technology, before achieving saturation levels in the cultures has had to go through two basic stages: first to be in stark evidence; second to be interiorized to the point of invisibility. For example, at first electrical wiring was much in evidence everywhere and many

Canadian cities are still plagued with rather ugly telephone poles and outside wiring, but the tendency, even if it costs much more, is to put it all underground.

The trend to discretion may, in some cases, come from a sort of self-regulated strategy. Electricity is going undercover, so to speak, not only because it partakes of the nature of the human nervous system, but also because a baseline technology works best when it remains unquestioned and undetected. Well-versed in such matters, McLuhan was fond of quoting Joyce's line in *Finnegans Wake*: "The viability of vicinals is invincible as long as they are invisible." A momentous example of this invisibility or transparency of the underlying medium ruling a culture is that of literacy. How long will it take for us to realize the formidable effects the alphabet has had on us since the Renaissance and the Reformation? Of course, as soon as we know how much our basic idea of ourselves has depended on this now less-dominant technology, we will change quite radically. A new generation of cyberdesigners might be called upon to redesign our psychology itself....

There is indeed a psychological change to be expected from the development and mass consumption of VR-related technologies. As they learn to use VR from kindergarten to the workplace and at home for evening and week-end entertainment, people will come to realize that all our technologies, especially the electronically based ones, are not simply external improvements in our immediate environments, but quasi-organic extensions of our most intimate being. VR's true nature is not merely to produce objects, but to extend and expand subjects. When design becomes the standard interface between thinking and doing, the activities that depend on thinking and planning can become direct extensions of thinking and feeling. As we invest our environment with our sensibility in VR, we are brought to the realization that this intelligent and sentient world we are wrapping around ourselves is but an extension of our own minds and souls.

CHAPTER NINE

ORAL VERSUS LITERATE LISTENING

Today our sight has dimmed; it no longer sees our future, having constructed a present made of abstraction, nonsense, and silence. Now we must learn to judge a society more by its sounds, by its arts, by its festivals, than by its statistics. By listening to noise, we can better understand where the folly of men and their calculations is leading us, and what hopes it is still possible to have.

– Jacques Attali[50]

Attali's book, *Noise: The Political Economy of Music,* describes how the economy of music has taken control over our sensibility and thus modulated significant aspects of our culture. It is an extremely perceptive inquiry into our cultural ground and into the predictive power we can derive from analyzing the music of our own time. In the excerpt quoted above, the author achieved his profound insight by opposing vision to hearing as an aspect of our present cultural and social predicament. Surprisingly, however, apart from a few observations about the impact of written music on the restructuring of musical genres and forms, there is no mention of the profound effect literacy has had upon our culture and especially upon our attitudes towards hearing. I say that it is surprising because the issue of written scores is a prime example of the kind of control literacy has taken over the psychodynamics of western people. From the Renaissance up to the recent reversal provoked by electronic technologies, the writing down of music has amounted to mastering sound and reducing to second class status all spontaneous popular forms or traditional folkloric rhythms. The opposition between writing and music is almost a biological one, as writing takes control of the brain while organized sound takes control of the whole body.

Generally, in dealing with our so-called "higher" senses, vision and hearing, we have the attitudes of producers, not consumers. We are perfectly content to use our nose and tastebuds for fun, but we look and listen for profit. Most hearing and listening in our urban environment is functional. Even recreational listening tends towards the functional end, as we go to jazz, classical, pop concerts "to relax," to tell ourselves and others that this is the time to stop and listen. Most of us go to concerts as we practise sports, dutifully (if we are not doing it professionally). Our use of touch is also a rational, puritanical affair, except in rather specialized and intimate circumstances. Yet, even in the context of public aesthetics, a difference must be drawn between looking and listening. We design things to look pleasing but we usually do not bother to make them sound pleasing. When it isn't given to whirring and purring and producing comical beeps, high technology's best compliment to the ear is to make its products silent and acoustically unobtrusive, which is the mark of efficiency. But our culture would sooner deafen us to undesirable sounds, than make such sounds less undesirable or turn them into pleasurable experiences. Children who grow up in the urban industrial cacophony have to create loud music to bring some coherence to all these sounds and smooth the hard, shrill, broken edges of glass, brick and steel.

The soundscape of the urban culture is a rich wasteland. Huge amounts of human energy get sucked into the black hole of the city, which regurgitates it as white noise. We get back raw energy from this white noise, but we lose our sensitivity to sound in the bargain. Of course we do not realize that we have lost anything because long ago we became accustomed to giving hearing an ancillary role. When a whole society suffers from hearing loss, there's nobody left to tell about the damage done. In the world of the deaf, the one who can hear is Joan of Arc, a madwoman. Our neglect of the ear may be one of the prices we have paid for literacy.

CAN MEDIA AFFECT OUR SENSORY MODES?

Close your eyes and imagine the world around you right now. If you are highly literate, the chances are that what rules your representation of this environment is a visual model. A box (the room) with things and a person inside. Perhaps there is someone else or a pet, in the box with you. Perhaps you can hear cars or birds outside your room. Now, if you are not so taken by the powers of literacy, you hear sounds that others do not notice. You can achieve a perfectly useful and manageable representation of your room by layering many levels of sounds: the rustling of your clothes, the ambient room sound, plumbing gurgles and furnace sounds. You can hear sounds as layered sculptures containing textures and designs, all bearing some kind of pressure upon you.

One experiment that I recommend to test the difference between oral and literate listening is to duck your head discreetly and close your eyes at your next crowded social gathering. You will be surprised at the number of different conversations you will be able to follow simultaneously. Then, open your eyes and try to keep it up. You will find it very difficult, if not impossible. The reason for that effect is twofold: first, your eyes take up a great deal of mental energy. Our sensory functions are selective. There is only so much energy that can go into a given situation for an efficient response. Survival is the prompter. Certain senses require more energy than others, such as vision, for instance, which requires eighteen times more energy than hearing. Second hand vision is both faster and more comprehensive than hearing, especially under our visuo-cultural conditions.

Because of their intuitive grasp of the tyranny of the eye, many symbolist poets from Verlaine to Claudel have recommended shutting one's eyes to become "a seer." But the main reason is probably that vision is obsessive and exclusive. The frontal view afforded by the eyes supports and encourages a specialization of attention that tends to eliminate any other perception. As Canadian composer Murray Shafer has suggested, with our eyes we are always at the edge of the world looking in, while with our ears, the world comes to us and we are always at the centre of it. Of course, this effect is the same for everybody from the jungle to the urban headhunter. But the frontal experience of visual concentration is also what is acquired, sometimes at the cost of great efforts, as one becomes literate. Thus literate people, who need to make and control their sense of everything, first trust their eyes before they even consider their ears. They also tend to concentrate their attention on the linear unfolding of events, conversations and situations, they have to "see it to believe it." However there may be a hidden neurobiological ground to our favouring one sensory ratio over another.

According to neurobiology, we grow into our environment not only anatomically, following genetic programming, but also neurologically, following cultural programming. Our brain, though initially geared to develop according to cross-culturally common programs, is gradually exposed to more and more exclusively cultural influences and conditioners that require selective responses and define the ratio of our sensory inputs in daily life. It is obvious that we hardly use our ears to find our way in an urban environment, whereas this is not true for those who have to live in the bush or the rain forest.

It may be that, as babies, even as neonates, we can all perceive a great variety of sounds. This much is borne out by the research of Toronto psychologist Sandra Trehub and others, which indicates that for a few hours and even days after birth, babies can differentiate between different languages.[51] This faculty seems to disappear quite soon, as the baby begins to settle in his or her maternal linguistic environment. Alfred Tomatis' theory that certain languages concentrate in preferred bandwidths[52] may be given some relevance here as neonates begin to specialize their attention for airborne linguistic sounds that reflect the frequency range of the language and the voice of their mother. The interesting feature of Trehub's work, however, is not that the babies' ears become attuned in a specialized way, but rather, that they very quickly lose the ability to accommodate other, non-relevant sounds.

French neurobiologist Jean-Pierre Changeux has developed a theory of "selective stabilization of synapses" to explain why we lose rather than gain sensory flexibility after exposure to consistent environmental stimulants. The suggestion is that the growth and development as well as fixation of neural connections in the brain and the central nervous system are conditional upon preferred use of certain patterns over others. We train our nervous system by habituation, just as an athlete trains his or her muscles.[53] Another way of looking at this process is to say with French linguist Jacques Mehler that, as we specialize "we learn by unlearning" other less appropriate responses.[54] It is as if we were carving our nervous system as well as our destiny while we were growing up.

Beyond our biologically and neurologically determined selection of listening and hearing patterns, there are cultural conditions that restrict the scope of our hearing to what is relevant to our specific social and psychological environment. If we are to give credit to Benjamin Lee Whorf's theories about the impact of our vocabulary in defining and limiting our psychological experience, there is a possibility that we only hear, or pay attention to those sounds that are described by the vocabulary (verbs, nouns, adjectives) and by the grammar (relationships) of our particular language. To wit, there are only two words, whether in French or in English, to describe the actions of listening and hearing, while there are dozens of verbs describing manners of looking (seeing, looking, perceiving, admiring, gazing at, glancing at, spying, and so on).

Even the way we use our own language can help to direct our psychological and, perhaps, our sensory experience. Neurolinguistic Programming (NLP), Bandler and Grinder's celebrated method of therapy, is partly based on the recognition that, as individuals, we privilege certain senses over others in our daily use of metaphors. There are those who insist on saying: "I see what you mean," in contrast to those who are content to acknowledge: "I hear you." NLP practitioners claim that those among us who show statistical consistency in choosing their sensory metaphors, with a bias in favour of visual metaphors, are likely to show better skill in that chosen sense than in the others.

Listening, in contrast to hearing, is a product of selective attention; it is driven not by inner processes but by outer ones. As a selective process, listening is switched "on" or "off." We switch to the listening mode for information and for taking stock of our environment. Even so, there are different kinds of listening: listening for words, for overt meaning, for hidden meaning, for emotions, for entertainment, for the self, for a global situation, for God, for meditating, etc. Each one of these listening functions requires a different set of attitudes, postures, expectations, judgements and storing and discarding measures. Each one can be called " a mode." We switch on one mode or another depending upon our circumstances and our need. As I suggested above, our cultural environment may prompt us to select one mode preferentially. I want here to emphasize the differences between two opposite modes, which for convenience, I will call the "oral" and the "literate" modes of listening.

The basic difference between the two modes is that oral listening tends to be global and comprehensive, while literate listening is specialized and selective. One is attending to concrete situations and to persons, whereas the other is interested in words and verbal meanings. One is context-bound, the other is relatively context-free. The first is cosmo-centric and spatial, the latter is linear, temporal and logocentric.

The ancient Greeks were acutely aware of the problems of perception and of their cultural consequences. Greek tragedy is nothing but the literary and dramatic response to new sensory conditions introduced by alphabetic literacy. However, the dramatists themselves did not know the real source of their predicament. When Tiresias tells Oedipus that he is blind to the truth of his position, what he is really implying is that Oedipus' excessive reliance upon his eyes and visual logic has made him blind—or, more accurately, deaf—to anything beyond the evidence. The fact is that, as western people, we have become gradually deaf through no fault of our own, through the rewiring of our nervous system by literacy.

HOW LITERACY TAKES OVER THE NERVOUS SYSTEM

In the beginning of his otherwise rather fanciful book on *The Origins of Consciousness in the Breakdown of the Bicameral Mind*, Julian Jaynes gives a perfect example of our tendency to conceptualize our own experience: he suggests that if you think back and reflect on the last time you were sitting in a bathtub, you almost automatically create a fiction: you imagine yourself, hardly defined, seen from a short distance, lying in a bath. But, of course, Jaynes points out that you have never experienced a bath in such a way, except maybe on a home movie made about you by someone else. You do not evoke the sensation of water around your waist—that would be an icon—you merely throw together the concept of yourself within the concept of a situation involving somebody taking a bath in a bathtub. You merely overlap your representations of your body and your particular bathtub, bona fide icons, into an otherwise generic concept.[55]

This is what a concept is, a mental representation, hardly an "image" at all, that contains little or no sensory information, but that has a great deal of adaptability to combine rapidly with other concepts or with icons, and even perceptions, to make sense. Now there is no reason to believe that any culture of the world is devoid of any of these categories of mental images. It would be silly to suggest that oral cultures are not capable of forming concepts, if only because concepts are the building blocks of language. Alison Gopnik, one of the cognitive scientists who did research at the McLuhan Program, has been studying the formation of concepts in early childhood and, from her work, there is little doubt that children begin to develop concepts long before they begin to read.

However, it is not silly to suggest that learning to read and write emphasizes the use of concepts over any other mental category. Why? Spoken words are nothing but concepts once they are written down and separated from their context. Whereas spoken words always bring up percepts and icons, written words are concepts in isolation, until they are combined into images by the reader. Literacy favours the use of concepts, merely by presenting speech in little units strung together. This makes for a conceptual use of language, even in live speech.

As people whose attitudes are ruled by literacy, we tend to listen for the meaning of words, rather than for the substance of an argument or for the intention of the speaker. This may not necessarily be the case for the oral listener.

ORAL LISTENING

On the other hand, as McLuhan has pointed out in *The Gutenberg Galaxy*, the "split between the eye and the ear," which is consequent to the diffusion of alphabetic literacy, can create strange difficulties in cultures that remain oral.[56] There is this true and delightful observation about a Turkish scribe who was the only person in a small coastal village who could read. Whenever he had to read private letters for his illiterate co-villagers, he would cover his ears with his hands, to show that he wasn't listening.

As a direct effect of the growth of literacy, the development of drama in classical Greece introduced a new social role and a new attitude: the hypocrite. *Upokritos* originally meant 'the answerer,' in fact, the 'actor,' but etymologically the word signifies 'the one who judges from beneath.' The hypocrites and the Pharisees of the new testament may be associated with the values of the learned people; That is, the literate. Pharisees were rich and therefore educated. Not only did they use their learning to interpret and turn the meanings of the sacred texts to their advantage, but they were known not to come up front on any issue, especially in confrontation with Christ. Everybody uses language for communication and control, but oral people may use it more for communication than control.

In *Orality and Literacy*, Walter Ong summed up many years of research into the comparison between the oral and the literate minds, suggesting several features of what he calls "the psychodynamics of orality." Each feature may correspond to a characteristic attitude in listening, namely what to listen for, how to listen, who to listen to and how to store or remember what has been heard.[57]

WORDS WEIGH WHAT
THE SPEAKER WEIGHS

First of all, in a truly oral culture, words are not cheap: the fool is the one who talks too much. Everything that is said carries weight either for you or against you, so you have to choose your words. In an oral culture, words are supported by the presence, the energy and the reputation of the speaker; they are the extension of his or her power and they exact attention from the listeners as measured against the eminence of the speaker. On the other hand, French anthropologist Marcel Mauss reminds us that the power of the speaker is really granted by the listeners, just as it is by the contemporary audience, well primed by promotion, public relations and the reputation of the performer, that gives power to the TV actor, the concert hall musician, or the politician.[58]

But oral words in a literate culture have little value. Even on paper, they can be cheap. It takes a great deal of procedural ritual to give weight to written words, such as in contracts, legal papers and decrees. While much of the power of oral words is given by their non-verbal markers, by itself the printed word does not yield any nonverbal information. Some unofficial research in university labs seems to indicate that, on the average, the total information content of ordinary human conversations went 7 percent to verbal material and 93 percent to non-verbal cues. The oral word is never unaccompanied. Intention and forcefulness are largely given to intonation, volume, scansion and other oral and tonal values. Print and billboard advertising are nothing if not attempts to recover the power and nuances of oral delivery in visual form.

In this regard we are presently witnessing a reversal; the words of a statesman on television are given weight not by their content, but by the image of the person who pronounces them. Another reversal is a tendency in contemporary law to pay attention to oral contract, in, for example, hiring, firing and promises of marriages. These changes are sure signs that we are returning to an oral culture or, more precisely, to an electronic oral culture.

ASSOCIATIVE LISTENING

The second feature proposed by Ong is that in an oral culture, "you only know what you can recall." Thus there is a heavy emphasis on memory, not merely the private memory of the speaker, but the collective memory of the audience. This kind of memory is contained, not outside the rememberer, but in the words, rhythms, gestures and performances of enacted recollections. In such a context, people are not terribly interested in new ideas or concepts, they listen for what they already know, much in the way we tend to look for recognizable features in new faces or new situations: "This reminds me of such event" or "This face reminds me of so and so."

Oral people are in a condition of permanent associative thinking, not in speculative or specific idea processing. Such a cognitive set-up is very conducive to analogies and myth formation. A myth can only work if it lends itself to many human situations and many interpretations without losing its basic structure. Another corollary to the psychodynamics of oral memory is that oral information tends to be shared collectively, rather than held in privately. Even the power associations of church and state in early medieval cultures were oligarchies of shared information. Private information ownership and control is one of the distinguishing features of a fully literate culture.

LISTENING WITH ONE'S BODY

Oral thought remains close to the human lifeworld and shuns abstractions. Oral listening searches for images rather than concepts, persons rather than names. Sense is made and organized around vivid images acting in context. The oral discourse is built around narratives and, as Havelock demonstrates in his analysis of early Greek literature, prefers verbs of action over predicates.[59] These figures are defined and opposed in agonistical tensions. Just as newscasters project drama, even when they have to report on unexciting budget decisions in the Commons, the oral listener will favor dynamic drama over static descriptions. Again, this tendency corroborates the suggestion that we first learn and make sense by body imitation. TV makes sense to the youngest child because it talks to the body, just as the mind works in its representations of reality, directly with images stored and borrowed from multisensory inputs in the total human nervous system.

THE SPACE BETWEEN: MEN AND WOMEN HEARING

A final selection among Ong's many relevant observations is his notion that oral thought is "empathetic and participatory rather than objectively distanced." The focus of oral listening is not so much the source of the voice as the space created between the interlocutors. The ego of oral people, though not absent (and sometimes highly expressive in case of loss of face) is generally much less personalized and, therefore, weaker than the ego of literate people. Without undue irreverence to women, the listening attitudes of oral people are participatory in a similar way to the manner that women listen. There is the fascinating research of Stanford Psychologist Diane McGuinness, who suggests that women are genetically conditioned, across all cultures, to respond better to hearing than to vision.[60] Men see twice as well as women, conversely women hear twice as well as men. This physical difference, adding itself to other more obvious ones, brings on a radically different attitude in men and women towards language. Men tend to consider language instrumentally, whereas women are more accustomed to speak relationally. The space between the speaker and the listener is where the oral culture's action is.

LITERATE LISTENING

Literate listening is a highly trained kind of *thinking*. As children we learn to think not only by reading and doing mental exercises and working a primer of logic, but by listening to the kind of formal, trained and structured talk of the classroom teacher. Thinking itself, for the literate person, is primarily structuring speech in the silence of one's mind. And, of course we find most models of structured speech in books, but it is found there as a static succession of statements. It is only when we are required to put together the words and sentences of a complex delivery from a teacher that we turn the static into dynamic forms.

A trained mind is a mind whose principal task is to eliminate noise, that is, unnecessary information, to make room for specialized responses. A mind trained by literacy is led to process information in thought rather than in action. While thinking the literate mind proceeds in words rather than images. Within those words and sentences the literate mind organizes itself in concepts rather than metaphors.

School itself is ruled by alphabetic literacy. Speech must yield information, not sensations; knowledge, not emotions; structure, not rhythms. The effect of the alphabet is to dry up human dialogue, to decontextualize it so as to make it available for re-use in other contexts. It is quite fitting that Plato's *Dialogues* have been turned into the highest tribute to the literate mind. What began as an oral experience in Socrates' encounters with his friends and entourage was laid down and mastered by writing, that is, decontextualized. One wonders what would have come out of a taped recording of Socrates.

Sylvia Scribner and Michael Cole did a ground-breaking study in the early eighties to demonstrate that the role played by the school was essential to distinguish between a so-called literate and an oral culture.[61] They suggested that the forms of formal instruction are what children, and even mature students, take home from the school situation. Indeed, formal literate speech is not merely a succession of words, it is also presented by a posture, a position and attitudes that are easy for a child to recognize and to adopt. In "real" life, nobody speaks like a professor, except, possibly, the newscaster on the radio. Still, the influence of the classroom teacher on our manner of listening is such that most of us go on to interpret the meanings of daily life speech with much of the legalistic, formal way we were trained to use when we were analyzing sentences in our grammar classes.

However, we do not gain instant access to the abstractions of our literate condition. We must first learn things in the context of the situation we are in. Jean-Marie Pradier's papers on the biology of the acting profession inform us that the great Japanese actor Zeami claimed that, in Japanese, "learning" really means to imitate with one's body.[62] We all begin that way. A child learns by gestures and imitation. It may be that it is easier for our nervous system to integrate information all at once by seeing, hearing and doing simultaneously, than by separating, sorting and storing specialized bits of information. It may even be more pleasurable: neurobiologists Michael Studdert-Kennedy and Myron Mishkin tell us that one of the most exciting tasks of the newborn is to coordinate sensations of different senses coming simultaneously. Even the two-year old's fun of banging a toy against the bars of the crib may come from the recognition that touching, hearing and seeing all come from the same gesture.

Now compare the situation of learning, listening with one's body, to that of reading. While reading the body is stilled, almost as that of someone asleep. The reader is either in silence, or has made sufficient reservations in his or her mind to turn the ambient noise into silence. That kind of control, by the way, bears witness to the power of literacy over our hearing. When we read, we literally "shut our ears" as if we had "earlids."

At first, turning written words into images is fairly hard work. I will never forget my father leaning over my shoulder to make sure that I was reading Alphonse Daudet's short story for children, "La chêvre de Monsieur Seguin." The sun was shining outside, and I could hear my friends playing with my brother in the garden. I was quite frustrated. "It's so easy," my father said, "all you have to do is to imagine a little white goat, going up a flowery mountain, running and munching all day and, at night, meeting a dark, fierce wolf, and fighting for her life." That was easy for him. He had seen plenty of goats, mountains, wolves maybe and he had read the story before, many times. I had seen goats too, and mountains, and I had seen pictures of wolves, but somehow I had to make a real effort to put it all together, because the images didn't seem to fit. They were wooden and flat, and all I wanted to do was to run outside with my friends. It is quite obvious to me that most kids like cartoons, comics and TV because they don't have to provide the images from their own minds.

I used to play improvisations on the recorder. I sometimes had the urge to let out miles of melodies stored in my body by prolonged exposure to classical music by my parents. Music must be stored in the body in the way long- and short-term memory stores it in the brain. Some kinds of music dissipate in seconds. Others remain a lifetime, stored in the limbs, or maybe the brain, or even the heart. When I played something that really worked, a strange thing would happen to my ears: right after I stopped playing, I would hear a buzzing sound echoing the size of the room, as if my ears had suddenly become a kind of sonar probing all my surroundings at once. Normally, my access to ambient noise is selective, not global. If I don't have a need for a sound, I don't hear it, unless it is very intrusive. But in this case, it was as if my playing had turned my body into a monitoring system designed to detect the expansion of being. I could hear more and deeper than usual. I thought it must be the reward of the musician. Needless to say, it was a great joy. I can't tell whether my improvisations worked because of this special quality of sound, or whether the special quality of sound only came because I played well. But one thing was certain, playing like that helped me to move completely from the literate to the oral mode. We all need that more than ever.

CHAPTER TEN

MEDIA AND GENDER

TAKING CONTROL
OF ONE'S INSIDES

UNTIL RECENTLY, the natural law of reproduction, child-bearing and education guided social conventions and maintained stability at the core of social life. The pill, of course, changed that. The pill's power as a symbol was more effective than its technological use: it was a kind of inverted weaning, not of children from mothers but of mothers from childbearing. Women do not "have" to bear children, they can "choose" to have them. In another few years, they will demand—and rightly so—to be paid to have them. Recent legal developments are in effect replacing the traditional patriarchy by matriarchy because women have now acquired the life-and-death power over their progeny once associated in early Roman law with men alone.

THE FAMILY AS AN ARTFORM

In the sixties, children became artforms, prime material for educational experiments from Montessori to Summerhill. Cut off at both ends from nature's control by law and technology, human life had become a commodity, a resource like all the others—although most people do not yet seem to realize this. Now the nuclear family itself has become an artform, whether for working or gay couples. In fact the word nuclear has become literally true: new childless families have two protons and no electrons! Two producers, no consumers! I have heard of childless couples who grace their condominium with a nursery, like a cultural vestige of a distant past.

BIOLOGY IS BUNK

Biology may have been "destiny" at one time but it certainly is not so anymore: until we learned to split the atom, crack the genetic code and harness electricity, humans were pretty well under the thumb of nature. Today, for better or for worse, we are learning to re-create nature—at own peril, of course—but henceforth unavoidably. This development, that makes cultural and gender relativism a necessity and not an option, greatly affects all arguments that would put women "back in the kitchen." Women today can compete success-fully with men, and even beat them, in the specialized job market. Today, for each man who begins a new enterprise, five women do so. The suspicion is growing that women may be better equipped to deal with our new situation than men are. This brings us back to biology, of course, but with a new twist: when biology meets culture, women arrive at the meeting place first.

SMOKING, GENDER AND THE SUPPRESSION OF THE BODY

Have you noticed that at parties and in public places today, more women than men are smoking? This in spite of the fact that smok-ing has become a public offence and an unfashionable sign of weak-ness, possibly revealing an immoral, suicidal streak in what outwardly appears to be a healthy body. Surely these young women know better than to try to impress people with their "liberated" stance by adopting a traditionally "male" vice? Smoking should not be taken lightly, not because it threatens your life, but because it, like alcohol, drugs, opium, pot, crack, cocaine and other ingestible or inhalable substances, takes control of your insides and is a sure indicator of large hidden social phenomena.

Beside screening the smoker from immediate and personal access, smoking, like alcohol, dulls the sensitivity of the body to enhance the abstractions of the mind. In excess, alcohol simply drowns the brain and makes it soggy, but nicotine dries it up. Women have begun to smoke for the same reason that men are stopping: each is meeting the other halfway: men are increasing their sensitivity by letting their bodies talk to them, while women are decreasing their sensitivity by reducing the volume of information their bodies naturally give them. Of course, to the extent that they drink and smoke, women get just as uptight and nervous as men used to be and consequently are suffering the same risks and rates of cancer and heart attacks. But the point of women smoking is that, in order to accept some of the hard psychological conditions of living in the "real world," it is imperative that they succeed in silencing their bodies.

HEARING VERSUS SEEING

Women are more sensitive than men to their own bodies because their attention is not specialized. Women probably do not focus their attention on one thing at a time the way men do. Women use their ears as much, if not more, than their eyes. This means that they are accustomed to staying in touch with many things at once, including their own physical responses to events around them. As I have noted, according to Diane McGuinness, women hear better than men. Their threshold of acoustic sensitivity is almost a full decibel lower than men's. Now seeing and hearing are not only different ways of accessing and processing information, they establish totally different relationships between ourselves and the environment.

Suppose you could associate women with hearing and men with seeing, what kinds of differences would you find in the way they interpret their environments? With their keen hunter's eyes, men would be on the look-out in the jungle, urban or natural, noticing or expecting any minute event requiring specialized attention for a specific purpose. Women don't have to go very far to know everything around them; their whole bodies tell them. They hear whole people, not just words, they hear situations, front and back, before and after. When I say they hear, I also mean they touch. Hearing and touching are very close. That is why women are much more sensitive than men to touching. The world of women has a rich texture of minute pressures that keep a balance between body and mind, between what they already know and what they must learn.

RELATIONAL VERSUS INSTRUMENTAL

Diane McGuinness adds that this hearing/seeing difference also affects men and women's attitudes to language. Men are trained by the attention they pay to what they see, to look for meaning alone in language. Women are trained by the attention to what they feel, to listen for contextual cues in what they are given to hear. McGuinness uses simple but powerful words: men have an *instrumental* attitude to language and life, while women have a *relational* bias towards words, sounds, people and things. Most of meaning is felt by women while most of meaning is thought by men.

THE STRENGTH OF WOMEN

Perhaps the reason why women are stronger than men, why they live, on average seven years more than men, is because they distribute their life stress evenly between their minds and their bodies. By recognizing and satisfying these two needs women put less wear and tear on their systems. However, as women increase their share of public responsibilities and fine tune their attention for specialized tasks, chances are that the gap of life expectancy between men and women will narrow.

This is not Harlequin romance biology, it is the recognition that women and men's ways of understanding the world are two equally important and complementary strategies of survival, and any serious loss of balance between the two threatens that survival. This is fundamental for the understanding of what gender is all about and what is happening to gender in our culture right now.

COSMOLOGY: "WHAT'S HAPPENING ANYWAY?"

Indeed we are making fewer children, but in a perverse sense we are also better at making them. Can we forget that in the seventeenth century, in no less protected a family than that of Louis, the King of France, it took four generations and countless stillbirths to produce a single, durable heir to the throne? There was a time when life was cheap in the West, as it is still in the Developing World. New satisfactions are in store for us to guide us along the paths of a global renewal.

CHAPTER ELEVEN

DEGREES OF REALITY IN THE MEDIA AND IN CULTURE

ATTACK ON REALITY

News item: "Reality ailing: experts believe illiteracy might be involved."

A T ONE TIME, you could trust reality. Plato and Aristotle had laid down the rules. If something didn't appear quite right, it was the fault of your inadequate sensory apparatus, not the world's. Despite Bishop Berkeley's grumblings about trees falling soundlessly in forests if nobody was there to hear them, reality was entrenched sometime during the eighteenth century by the German philosopher Immanuel Kant. As we shall see shortly, it was a product of the literate bias. Literature also reinforced this bias. Beside supporting the idea of reality by proposing an alternative, the job of fiction was to provide models for people to deal with reality. But reality was to be short-lived. For example, Realism, a nineteenth-century artistic movement that accompanied the rise of photography, is generally believed to be a reaction to the excesses of Romanticism. But I think that it had more to do with a bourgeois society coming to terms with the eerie comfort of early industrialization. Realism and Naturalism in art and literature were meant to reassure the public that there was a reality out there and the more unpleasant, the more real.

At a time when the world was real, the purpose of all scientific investigation was to describe a stable and reliable universe, with or without the help of God. Plato and Herodotus made reality real when they requested that facts replace opinions *(doxa)* in arguments and historical analysis. The atom was invented by another ancient Greek to put the universe on a solid material basis. As long as the atom held on, reality would be reliable. But even atoms cannot be trusted anymore. Today we know that atoms are very unreliable and we are all the more susceptible to ideas such as Schroedinger's who suggested that in quantum physics, "things are not, they only tend to be." Today it seems that the purpose of much scientific investigation is to mine the deep resources of our technological gullibility.

Since Einstein, Niels Bohr, Heisenberg, Freud and television, reality has been disintegrating rapidly. Today it is falling apart. The self and the soul are all over the place and God is not always around to put it all together. Emulating the Beatles, physicist and theorist David Bohm is hard at metaphysical work to show that yes, it's true, it's all in your mind.

Not long ago, even Coca-Cola was real. If the world was once real, why isn't it so anymore ?

REALITY TO FANTASY

Need I remind anyone after McLuhan or Postman or Meyrowitz or Bill Moyers, that "news is entertainment"? However, people believe that the news is for real, and they believe that TV news is the most real. The only time we do not feel guilty about watching TV is when we are watching the news, because we are doing our citizens' duty. Of course TV news is packaged like anything else on TV. *The World is Watching*, Peter Raymont's remarkable film about the way significant events in Nicaragua were reported by the networks, demonstrated newscasting biases in the processing of reality. The gist of Raymont's argument was that while ABC's crew was preparing a spot on the return of President Daniel Ortega from Moscow to Managua, they predicted—and were prepared to say—that he would declare at a major press conference at 5 PM that day that he would not negotiate with the Contras. The press conference was delayed until 7 PM, too late to make the 7 PM news in New York. The ABC crew went ahead with their planned footage, stating that Ortega stood firm on his position, only to discover, to their dismay, that Ortega had changed his mind on this fundamental issue. This incident may be interpreted as a problem in TV time management; however, in the course of his documentary, Raymont demonstrates many other convincing examples of message manipulation to fit the constraints of the medium. Television presents only "the news that fits" and if it doesn't fit, the producers will make sure it does.

Raymont's documentary is a sort of "reality concentrate" that can be paraphrased in what can be called the Law of Diminishing Reality. Reality vanishes by degrees in the following order:

1. live coverage
2. delayed live coverage
3. packaged news item
4. "objective" documentary
5. "point-of-view" documentary
6. "docudrama"

In principle, manipulation by the media is legitimized by the necessities of brevity and the need to cover an increasing number of important items in as short a time as possible. But it opens the way for a series of new reality frauds. For example, Ted Koppel's remarkable TV report, "Revolution in a Box," shows that what was presented to the American public as an aerial shot of Chernobyl right after the blow-up was, in reality, stock footage showing a rather peaceful, if misty and smoky, factory in the Po Valley, Italy. Another example in the same documentary shows the complete footage of a video of hostages "confessing" to conspiracy to escape a Middle East prison, demonstrating how the selection of appropriate excerpts and studio editing led to the fabrication of a "confession."

In these instances there was clear evidence of fraud, but what about ABC's famed "reconstructions"? If you happen to turn on your set while a re-enacted crime and the process of its investigation are being aired, you might take it for the real thing. This happened once when a clever viewer accused one of the actors in a re-enactment for his alleged part in the actual crime, because the viewer thought that he had spotted on the show something that proved his guilt!

In all these cases, the audience is liable to be caught in a trap more powerful that the reality effect of still photography. McLuhan's famous law, in these cases, may have to be rewritten: the context, not only the medium, is the message. . . It is as if a "reality detector mechanism" was fooled by the framing of the newsclip and we adopted a suspension of disbelief in reverse. With reality like this, who needs fiction ?

CHAPTER TWELVE

MASS, SPEED AND CYBERCULTURE

"Information expands as it's used. It's transportable at the speed of light. Above all, it leaks; it has an inherent tendency to leak."
– Harlan Cleveland

PSYCHOTECHNOLOGIES

THE GROWTH of psychotechnologies and information-processing has gradually shifted from the private universe of mind to the public world of the cathode ray tube. Because the video screen substitutes for the mind when it comes to image and information-processing, every era, along with the media that dominated that era, has corresponded to postural changes in our relationship with the video screen. Our one-way, frontal relationship with the TV screen ushered in mass culture. The computer screen, introducing two-way interactive modalities, added speed. The effect of integrated hypermedia will be total immersion. We are at the brink of a new depth culture which is now taking shape during the nineties. Every time the emphasis on a given medium changes, the whole culture shifts.

MASS

To get an idea of the total field created by television, imagine the whole nation mesmerized in front of the TV set at prime time, receiving information without responding. The only way the audience can impact the medium is through polls, buying patterns and surveys. With a broadcast medium, the energy pattern goes one way, into the receiver, where it is consumed with minimal resistance. This creates favourable conditions for the promotion and distribution of products, where the emphasis is on persuasion and packaging. Indeed, the heyday of the television era was also the time of unlimited advertising. The content of advertising was also the content of a new kind of collective consciousness, the active information that formed and informed the mainstream of North American and European culture.

In this way, the period of the mid-sixties to the mid-seventies was defined by mass culture. It began with the electron beam scanner painting light on our nervous systems, flooding our sensibilities with inflationary expansionism and aggressive marketing. The TV era saw unbridled world travel for graduating students, psychedelic trips for those who stayed home, overnight sensitivity-training schools, macrobiotics and psychotherapeutic methods, East-meets-West fantasies, sabbaticals for executives and, even, a new freedom for language myth-creation. All features of those exciting and idealistic times during the heyday of mass culture.

SPEED

The generous and expansive mental framework of the sixties was eventually checked by the limits-of-growth psychology of the early seventies, brought on by computerized rationalizations of the planet's exhaustible resources. The new pulse that started the shift of the seventies seems to have begun at the Hudson Institute with Herman Kahn's dismal projections of the Earth's natural energy supplies.

That was the work of rather clumsy mainframe computers. With the introduction of personal and portable micro-computers, which had penetrated domestic markets by the eighties, consumers were prompted to become producers. The new technology had changed our one-way relationship with TV to the two-way, interactive mode of personal computers. Computer screens established an interface between biological and technological electricity, between the user and the networks.

TV had made happy-go-lucky hippies of most of America's youth, firing photons into their willing brains. However, as they learned to talk back to their screens with computers, zappers, video recorders and camcorders, very young men and women recovered enough autonomy to forgo automatic reflex consumerism and quickly became successful entrepreneurs. The eighties saw the rise of "speed culture" and networking. Even as early as the late seventies, prescriptive disco music was shaping time with the hertz clock of its synthesizers, the "soul" of the new machines. Speed culture, culminating in the universal distribution of fax machines, whipped us into shape, streamlining business operations and going high-tech in style and content. Hippies were replaced by yuppies.

CYBERCULTURE

Now, as we penetrate the screen's virtual realities with eyephones, datagloves and datasuits, we are entering the third media era: Cyberculture. Cyberculture is the product of the multiplication of mass by speed, as video technologies are intensified by computer technologies. High Definition Television is a typical example of this kind of multiplication. The deeper message of HDTV is not better definition or finer resolution, but more power to the frame. HDTV is television educated by computer. HDTV is composed of millions of interactive pixels. Each pixel can be addressed for a specific command. The HDTV image is a sort of electronic dendritic system composed of millions of parallel processors. Before the end of the decade, we will see experiments combining HDTV and neural networks for enormously complex, educable operating systems.

We are discovering that there is as much room in inner space as in outer space. We are already exploring, industrializing and marketing the infinitely small realms of genetic, atomic and molecular fields. Yuppies are gone, cyberpunks are here. Business in cyberspace is mostly on-line, involving number-crunching, neural networks and expert systems, but it is also highly personalized as the new executives must learn to deal with the complexities of other cultural sensibilities. Cyberculture will seek and find valuable information from other societies. Western technologies are extending to meet with every culture on the planet. But electricity, though developed by western technology, is in spirit and in fact closer to eastern than western psychology. Hence, the value of exploring the integral psychological grounds of countries such as Japan, India or China.

PATTERNS OF MASS, SPEED AND CYBERCULTURE BEFORE AND AFTER 1980

"When information moves at electric speed, the world of trends and rumours becomes the 'real' world."

– Marshall McLuhan

It is difficult to remember the sixties. Grace Slick, lead singer of the Jefferson Airplane rock band, once said that anybody who claimed to remember the sixties couldn't possibly have been there. Indeed, memories of a time outside of time, a kind of unfolding eternal present, quickly receded after the oil crisis of the seventies. Now it seems as if we can hardly get past the mind-set of the eighties. We see the sixties darkly, through the lens of the eighties.

Did affluence really generate sixties' social trends or was it the other way around? Did the social trends promote the business trends? Did recessions and see-sawing bull and bear markets bring on a deficit economy? What happened to turn kids from hippies into yuppies? Historically, both free enterprise and Marxist ideologies have shared a tendency to look to the bottom line for the explanation of human and market behaviour. But that is too obvious to be useful. If other major variables were not also in play, we would see a situation where the bottom line did actually work, and efficiency would be its proof. We know this is not the case. Something other than human greed must be at work. My answer is that a deeper ground must be found, something that binds all the characteristics together.

BUSINESS TRENDS FROM THE EARLY SIXTIES TO THE EIGHTIES

The following charts may help. It is often revealing—and I hope, exciting—to look at before and after pictures. The table on page 128 compares the major business trends of the eighties to those of the sixties and mid-seventies (when the mythology of limits to growth hit business and government with the prospect of limited energy resources). Many of these trends need no introduction. They're known to anyone who was in business at the time. The real reason for bringing them together is to point out the consistency of the periods. It is relatively easy to see patterns unfolding, because the characteristics of each period rarely overlap. Another purpose of these charts is to provide some preliminary pointers for analyzing the behaviour of techno-magnetic fields. Contrary to what economists would have us believe, business trends often reflect conditions and circumstances beyond their control Finally, at the very least, there must be some kind of interdependence between business and social trends.

Table 1
BUSINESS TRENDS

	1960s–70s	1980s
Rising Economic Power	United States	Japan
Overall Structural Tendency	Expansion *(branches and franchises)*	Contraction *(mergers and acquisitions)*
Dominant Financial Mythology	Inflation	Deficit
Preferred Hardware	Planes and Automobiles *(transport)*	Computer *(communication)*
Role of Government	Centralization *(welfare)*	Deregulation *(privatization)*
Dominant Pattern of Investment	Blue chip and venture	Real estate and mutual funds
Dominant Business Ideology	Keynesian economics *(buying power stimulates economy)*	Reaganomics *(business knows best)*
Dominant Pattern of Internationalism	Multinationals *(single-item industries, many countries)*	Multisectorial *(diversification)*

What I call mythology is not necessarily something untrue, but something that, for one reason or another, grabs everybody's attention and becomes a source of consensual buzzwords. There is no need to prove that Japan is currently the rising star of the business world, or that we have just seen a rash of mergers, leveraged buy-outs and acquisitions. Government-against-deficit has replaced the government-by-deficit strategies of the seventies. The surgical cuts in social programs that accompanied Reaganomics have all but eliminated the welfare state policies of more liberal governments, at least in the English-speaking world.

SOCIAL TRENDS

When you look at the second chart, you'll want to ask yourself which came first, the social or the business trend. Indeed, that is a good question. People often say that the reason we went so cheerfully through the sixties was that there was a lot of money going around. And with less pressure to fight for a living, the baby boomers were given the chance to relax. In fact, there is much more money going around today. According to Joseph N. Pelton, "close to a hundred trillion dollars worth of global electronic fund transfers take place via satellite or cable each year."[63] Why is it then, that with more money than ever, in more places, we are asked by administrations in government, education, the arts and, of course, the social services, to tighten our belts and get ready for further, even more severe budget restrictions in future?

In the late seventies, almost overnight, and without so much as a prompting from government or education authorities, high-school kids and university students—if not their parents—stopped dropping acid and smoking dope. Why then and not sooner? Why did so many people stop smoking cigarettes during the eighties (with the possible exception of young, urban, professional women)? How do we explain the mainstream interest in the environment now registering over 80 percent in the polls, compared to the self-absorbed navel-gazing of the seventies? At the same time, in what would appear to be contradictory trends, yuppies have been pushing back the moment of having children as long as possible, and are more concerned with running for fitness than for office. Surely all this has little to do with Sony buying CBS, or the Reagan and Thatcher cuts to social programs? As you explore the validity and the relevance of Table 2, you may want to start looking for a techno-cultural field.

Table 2
SOCIAL TRENDS

1960s–70s	1980s
Producerism	Consumerism
Self-centredness *(me-decade)*	Environmentalism
Relationships	Fitness
Hippies	Yuppies
Feminism	DINKS *(double-income-no-kids)*
Social (and not-so-social) drugs	Non-smokers
Ideological drive	Bottom-line

PSYCHOLOGICAL TRENDS

The next chart tries to relate major changes not to the economy, but to the information-processing media that exerted a kind of hegemony over the culture, fashions and business attitudes of the time. TV had the power to relax and coax our sensibility into an expansive mood while computers contracted much of that expansive mood into tight, sharp minds and controlled emotions.

Television and computers conquered the industrial world, carving and shaping the corporate psychology according to their own highly distinctive criteria which, in turn, formed and informed distinctive policies within the culture that helped to develop others.

Table 3
PSYCHOLOGICAL TRENDS

	Television *(saturation during 70s)*	Computer *(penetration during 80s)*
Dominant Concepts	Mass culture Mass production Being everywhere at once	Speed culture Instant communication Being here and now where it counts
Main Patterns of Communication	Broadcasting (one-way) *(Give people what they want)*	Networking (two-way) *(Find out what people want)*
Dominant Marketing Attitudes	Seduction	Precision
Dominant Business Strategy	Promoting	Accounting
Main Sources of Metaphors	Body-senses-touch *(Touch me, feel me)*	Brain/central nervous system *(The Soul of the New Machine)*
Favourite Buzzwords	Myths, icons, images	Logic, AI, expert systems
Popular Mythological Representation	Superman *(X-ray vision, flying)*	*2001's* HAL *(command and control)*

If you replace the category headings in the first two charts by *Television* on the left and *Computer* on the right, you will be surprised that the new headings actually yield more information. They make even more sense than the classification by periods. TV turned us into inveterate consumers, by bringing the outside world inside our homes, inside the self. We developed a kind of voracious appetite for images and goods. But computers, by projecting outwards from our central nervous systems, giving us access and power over any point in the environment, at any time, for any purpose, made producers of us. The younger generation of men and women got high on small businesses and new ventures instead of drugs. The computerization of the economy is also key to all the other changes, being the nerve centre of the present body politic.

MASS HUMAN
VERSUS SPEED HUMAN

Mass man was homogenized and quite depersonalized. The speed man or woman of computerland reacts to people and emphasizes differences. And the reason for that is clear: whereas the mass man of television was surrounded by broadcast media networks, trapped in a world made for him by the consciousness industries, the speed man of computers is everywhere at the centre of things. Even the country policeman who catches you speeding on a back road can get access to your records by calling the force's data bank on his cellular phone. The new situation is quite paradoxical: as everything accelerates around him, speed man can afford to slow down. At the centre of things, speed men and women do not move. Their speed is the instant access they have to things and to information. Speed people are not principally consumers but producers and agents. Their production and their actions are marked by their personal character.

Television created the notion of the "mass man" and the idea of mass media. We had no idea that there were such things as "mass consumption" and "mass psychology" until television revealed them to us. But computers brought in the "speed culture." The computer is not a mass medium, but a personal one, as in personal computer. We have been driven by the need to simultaneously accelerate and humanize the interaction between ourselves and our machines. Take, for example, the attempt to create voice-operated systems, or the drive for user-friendliness. The best software designers are asked to elaborate programs that will understand natural languages in as many combinations as possible. The dream of the ultimate translating machine, of efficient "fuzzy-functions" and of simultaneous multiple processing is fuelled by ever-increasing technological possibilities.

BUSINESS STRATEGIES

Most of the trends in the psychological trends chart deserve further elaboration, which will be the subject of the next chapters. Meanwhile, let's see what a techno-cultural field survey can say about business attitudes. Table 4 compares the business generation strategies of the sixties and seventies to the recent techniques of the eighties. Again, television in the sixties and computers in the eighties seem to have acted as magnets with different polarities.

One of the most significant changes in business attitudes during the eighties was the new emphasis placed on psychographics, in contrast to demographics, which had ruled the sixties and the seventies. This was clearly a shift from mass to speed psychology effected by computers. The change enabled industry to become precise in statistical and trend analyses under the pressure of increasing competition for the leading edge. Psychographics allowed marketing executives to figure out much more than numbers. It was a qualitative jump in audience research, which made psychological rather than numerical data the indicator of potential growth areas in the market. Computer-assisted research can pinpoint with even greater precision what kinds of people are likely to buy a product or a service, how much they will buy, for how long and where they are located. Several market-research companies are now busy creating their own categories of people under various classifications. New collective personae, representing market-worthy segments of the total population, are being defined not in terms of character, as were individual men and women by writers and social critics after the Renaissance, but in terms of reliable buying habits shown by tastes, dispositions and attitudes.

Table 4
BUSINESS STRATEGIES

1960s – 1970s	1980s
Mass markets	Speed markets
Demographics	Psychographics
(*large numbers*)	(*the right numbers*)
Marketing by advertising	Niche marketing
Planned obsolescence	Upgrading
Packaging	Positioning
(*the package is the message*)	(*keeping tabs*)
Overstaffing	Downsizing
	(*streamlining*)
Public relations	Business communications
Emphasis on product	Emphasis on audience
Trial and error	Trend analysis
Campaigning	Spin-doctoring
(*military operations*)	(*let the force do it*)
Show and sell	Polls
	(*statistics*)

CATCH PHRASES

There's a quick method to get to the deeper structure of any contemporary situation. When you want to get an angle on what is going on, check the current buzzwords; government, business and the media are very fond of them. Buzzwords reveal the afterimages of social change; they exactly represent huge powers of social change. Whenever a new buzzword or catch phrase arises, you can be quite sure that its appearance depends on some area of activity in a techno-cultural field.

Computers, for example, have given rise to a great number of buzzwords, or afterimages, even as they were shifting the ground of everyday life. Some of these words or phrases are obviously related to computers: networking, interfacing, interactive, user-friendly, and so on. Other afterimages are not so obviously related to computers, but they have been given a new level of prominence because of them: downsizing, crisis management, cost-benefit-analysis, psycho-graphics, personal touch, fitness craze, internalizing, cocooning and anti-smoking. Buzzwords are usually verbs and/or nouns implying action and thus often reveal interesting hidden cultural changes in the business community.

CYBERCULTURE
IN THE NINETIES

At this point in the nineties, the dominant buzzword is unquestionably "globalization." When McLuhan first introduced the notion of the "global village" back in the early sixties, people didn't really pay attention. Japan was still producing cheap cameras and small cars, the Berlin Wall had just been raised and China hadn't even begun to wake up. Telecommunications were very expensive and only accessible to the privileged few. People would make jokes about the famous "hot line" between Moscow and Washington, an exotic device fraught with the ominous task of announcing the nuclear holocaust. I remember wondering whether Nikita Khrushchev would have been concerned about international telephone charges before calling John Kennedy about the Bay of Pigs incident.[64]

GLOBAL TRANSPARENCY

The democratization and proliferation of instant communications and personal telecommunication devices have replaced our previously opaque and distant feeling about the planet with a new sense of its immediacy and transparency. What boundaries exist for electricity? The world's telephone lines are open. We witnessed the 1989 Chinese student uprising on television while fax machines reported Beijing news in spite of intense government controls. Twenty thousand miles up in the air, over 3,000 communication satellites are relaying information to dishes all over the world. Within hours of the comet Shoemaker Levy Strauss 9's collision with Jupiter, images of the explosions were available on the Internet. Wire news networks are open to be received off the air, on-line or in print within or without a press agency. And even the data banks are open—for any clever hack who knows how to fool the system. Nobody can keep a secret for any length of time.

Today, only strict military control of media reporting, such as we experienced during the Gulf war, can effectively impede the scrutiny of everything by everybody. But even during the Gulf War, television viewers watched Scud missiles explode in Tel Aviv while commentators under strict military control were claiming none had struck the city. The opening up of eastern European countries, along with the erosion of communist control, is the one of the most powerful and stunning expressions of the effect of electronic technologies generating a worldwide glasnost.

REAL-TIME

There's something else that contributes to global opening up. The gap between communication stimulation and response is narrowing dramatically, increasing the quantity of transactions. There used to be a time when it took longer to send information than to collect it. Not anymore. In some businesses, the morning news is obsolete by lunch time. Consequently, we find business people obsessed with increasing the speed of access to their home, office and offshore contacts. Fax machines and cellular phones have found their way into cars and onto laps in airplanes, along with laptop computers. More and more people carry beepers, either to remind them of baby's next bottle or to go to the next phone booth to call the office or the clinic. The narrowing gap between action and reaction is creating a kind of continuity between planning and executing in "real-time."

On the other hand, the multiplication of contacts reduces local resistance to change. Upgrading the speed of action and reaction everywhere opens up the possibility of rapidly unifying responses all over the world. Today, whole societies and large scale economies, under the umbrella of single holding companies, are processed instantaneously as if they were single users of the electronic environment. Electricity surrounds the globe in a single mesh. Media weave one single tactile blanket of electrostatic activity around the planet. Any ripple in a stock exchange affects the delicate and sensitive balance of investments worldwide. Computers react immediately, while investors keep their eyes glued to their terminals. For some, it can be a matter of life and death. The news that the NYSE had crashed on October 19, 1987, reverberated instantly around the world, like whiplash.

The paradox is this. Our hardware—the material reality of the Earth—is contracting and imploding upon itself, because our technologies continually reduce the time and space intervals between operations. Meanwhile our software, our psychological and technological reality, is continually expanding. Access to the infinite realms—atomic and sub-atomic, planetary and galactic information structures—is also expanding the reaches of our on-going, "depth culture."

WHAT IS CYBERCULTURE?

Cyberculture is the result of the multiplication of mass by speed. Even as TV and radio bring us news and information en masse from all over the world, probing technologies, such as telephone and computer networks, allow us to go instantly to any point and inter-act with that point. This is the "depth" quality, the possibility of "touching" that point and having a demonstrable effect upon it via our electronic extensions. We can now do this in any context in the world and even beyond, since we have been sent numerous satellite probes into outer space. Today, from the Pioneer satellite, millions of miles away, we can receive a two-dimensional image of the surface of Miranda (one of the moons of Uranus) and render it in 3-dimen-sional relief by computer. The 3-D effect is only one expression of depth. The other is the literal depth of the probing itself. We are not content with surfaces anymore. We are even trying to penetrate the impenetrable, the video screen. A literal expression of cyberculture is the growing industry of virtual reality machines that allow us to pen-etrate the world of the video and computer screen and probe the endless depth of human creativity in science, art and technology.

Another expression of cybercultural depth is the penetration, by electronically assisted microscopes and nuclear-magnetic resonance devices into the infinitely small realms of molecular, genetic and atomic structures. Many technologies invite us to probe beneath the surface of the visible, or what is made visible by simulation or enlargement. These worlds were never accessible before. These realms, for which we are already building micro-structures and atomic motors, are becoming insatiable markets for manufacturing.

Cyberculture implies "seeing through." We see through matter, space and time with our information-retrieval techniques. When-ever a technology gives us mental and physical access to somewhere on the Earth or deep in space, beyond any previous limit, our minds follow. Hence our psychology must evolve with that technology. When we travel physically on business or pleasure, we are contained in the global sphere. However, when we think globally and send or receive information from our offices, we contain the Earth in our minds and in our networks. The information that we apply to this inner structure is part of a global thought and a global activity. As a form of expansion of the mind and frame of reference, globalization is one of the psychological conditions of cyberculture.

GLOBALIZATION IS PRIMARILY AN ISSUE OF PSYCHOLOGY NOT ECONOMY

Multinationals are like the idea of God during the Renaissance. Their centre is everywhere and their periphery nowhere. The consequence of all this is that the culture of business is becoming global culture itself. However, the rash of mergers and take-overs, the reconfiguration of local economies into global structures, supported by free trade agreements the world over, is not just a matter of good economic sense. Such developments could be considered in a different and, ultimately, more interesting light. Could the economy be considered as the comprehensive medium whereby society achieves its own integration on a new psychological—or psychotechnological—basis?

For example, the print and electronic media get very excited about monumental mergers and acquisitions. Take for instance the merger between Warner and Time, or the dramatic take-overs of traditional American firms by Japanese ones. Some people think this is all about sharp corporate affairs businesspeople and heavy-hitting lawyers reaping megabucks. But there are many other factors to consider. It is clear that instant information retrieval systems allow businesses to keep tabs on ever larger and even more complex realms of production, distribution and transaction. It is also clear that computerization supports and enhances the controls exercised by any government or administration that adopts it. However, we think naïvely that business and government promote computerization in the interests of efficiency or competition. But as it happens, most business executives initiated computerization on a hunch, or to keep up with the plant next door. Some have even found, to their dismay, that computerization, by dint of its complexity, actually slowed down business operations for a while.

So, it may be the other way around. Psychotechnologies like computer and video networks may be using business and government to proliferate. Psychotechnologies are intelligent machines developed by intelligent collectives and sold by aggressive sales forces. They are worked out at the interface of human invention, institutional support and basic need. Hence, one could conceivably suppose that computerization uses business and government as the ideal milieu for growth and integration.

CHAPTER THIRTEEN

ANALOGUE AND DIGITAL MINDFRAMES

NEW TRENDS IN COMPUTING

"In this electric age we see ourselves being translated more and more into the form of information, moving toward the technological extension of consciousness."

– Marshall McLuhan

DID A COMPUTER SEARCH YOUR BAG AT THE AIRPORT?

Airplane luggage in New York, Miami, and London airports goes through an unusually rigorous inspection before being loaded in the cargo bay. In addition to x-raying the bags for metal weapons, these airports use neural networks to screen for plastic explosives. The detection system bombards the luggage with neutrons and monitors the gamma rays that come flying out in response. The neural network analyses the signal and decides whether it came from an explosive.[65]

*T*ECHNOLOGY REVIEW contributor Herb Brody goes on to say "that's a difficult distinction to make. Different chemical elements release different frequencies of gamma rays. Explosive materials are rich in nitrogen, so an abundance of gamma rays at nitrogen's frequency raises suspicion. But some benign substances—including protein-rich materials such as wool and leather—also contain a lot of nitrogen."[66]

The beauty of the system is that, although neural networks aren't 100 percent accurate, their "search-and-decide" capacity can be calibrated to ensure that no real possibility will be overlooked and that there'll only be a 2 percent chance of a false alarm. Processing an average of 700 bags per hour, it saves a lot of time and grief for passengers and security people.

Neural networks have been in research and development for the last five or so years and many applications are now being commercialized. Neural networks represent a radically new departure in computer technology. It is a new generation of computer intelligence bringing us ever closer to emulating the human brain.

WHAT IS A NEURAL NETWORK?

According to J. Clarke Smith, Chief Financial Officer of the Sears Mortgage Corporation, "understanding how neural networks work is a job for Superman . . . any CFO, or even CEO, risks falling behind the competition race without at least a rudimentary knowledge of what neural networks are and just how they might be applied."[67] Artificial neural networks (ANN)—in contrast to the biological ones in the brain (BNN)—are made up of computer nodes, called "neurodes," that are flexibly interconnected. Unlike ordinary computers, which address coded numbers and compile them very fast, one by one, ANNs process information more like the human brain, by organizing patterns of weighted connections between their neurodes. "Weighting" a connection is equivalent to giving it more importance, relative to other, less-travelled relationships between variables. Maureen Caudill, one of the first consultants on neural networks, says that "a neural network learns by example; that is, it modifies the weights of the interconnections between the neurodes."[68] As Herb Brody explains it:

> Each neurode takes many input values, multiplies each by a "weighting" factor, adds together the products of these multiplications and mathematically operates on this sum to produce another set of values. These numbers may translate directly into an answer—say, the identity of a spoken word or a written character. More complex systems channel the outputs from one set of neurodes to many other neurodes, again through weighted interconnects. The network adapts and learns by varying the connection weights.[69]

Let's say that the desired output is a verdict on a mortgage loan decision. Each variable, such as the condition, market-value or location of the property, along with the financial resources and track record of the candidate, is addressed to a specific neurode that computes inputs by category. The job of the neural network is to build the pattern of interconnections that leads to the desired output, in this case, acceptance or refusal of a loan. The network won't succeed at the first attempt. It must go over the connections again and again to find out which combination is the most appropriate. This is where weighting comes in. Before it can make reliable decisions, the neural network must be exposed to hundreds if not thousands of different configurations of variables. Eventually, by self-adjusting its weighting for each new case, the network gathers enough "experience" to present the definitive recommendations. This is the way *we* think, isn't it?

IS NEURAL NETWORK A MISNOMER?

Upon reading the word 'brain' paired with 'computer,' many people experience an understandable irritation. This is partly because they have seen it too many times; partly because the issue of whether a computer is—or one day really will be—like a brain has not been resolved by the endless controversies. But does it matter whether we prove or disprove that the computer can think, or has a soul, or whatever fanciful definition some neuro-philosopher dreams up?

In spite of controversy, the metaphor must be powerful because it sticks. And there are good reasons to keep up the comparison. Herb Brody makes a convincing case for maintaining the relationship:

1. "The brain gets its power not from the speed of its individual switches but from the way they are linked together; it is the complex interconnection of these neurons that gives the brain the crucial ability to recognize patterns—and hence to learn."[70]
2. "As in the brain, an artificial neural network is constructed of simple components."
3. "Unlike most computers, a neural network learns from its mistakes."[71]

Again, in an attempt to draw the line between ANNs and BNNs, another researcher proposed "where neural systems are inherently analogue, electronic systems have been digital. Where neural systems are parallel in nature, electronic systems are generally serial."[72] In less than three years, this distinction has been rendered invalid by the invention of analogue chips.

ANALOGUE CHIPS

Analogue chips are very different from the usual digital chips. The now familiar vocabulary of bits and bytes does not apply here. Their way of processing data is neither "stop-and-go" nor sequential, but continuous.

They store information as a continuous range of values, typically as voltages in a capacitor, rather than as the binary 1's and 0's signified by a transistor's on/off switches. Since the inputs to a neural network are often analogue values—the brightness of a pixel, say, or the strength of a sound signal—analogue chips offer a fast, albeit less precise, computing short-cut. Neural-network integrated-circuit chips are now available commercially.[73]

Analogue chips are incredibly fast. "By encoding weights as voltages on a chip, neural networks can operate much faster than when they rely on software in a conventional computer. Engineers measure the speed of these in terms of 'connections' per second—about 10,000 times faster than is possible using conventional hardware."[74] If the technological thrust that supported conventional computers is applied with the same force to this new analogue generation, it is conceivable that new information-processing models will be borrowed directly from the brain. What is happening right now, in research centres around the world, is a kind of intensified dialogue between computer technology and the brain, where each party influences the growth and the understanding of the other.

NEURAL DARWINISM

Probably the most ambitious research project into neuro-biological models is that of 1972 Nobel Prize winner Gerald Edelman at Rockefeller University. His project is called Darwin III, and involves a complex neural network consisting of layers and layers of interconnections between sensory, motor and cognitive operations. It includes an eye, a robotic arm and a brainlike neural net. Edelman has coined the expression, "Neural Darwinism" to support his theory that neural connectors actually compete with each other to find and keep their place in the network.

To test the dynamics of such a theory, which is not unlike Chargeux's "selective stabilization of synapses," Edelman has built Darwin III in such a fashion that the artificial neural network connections of his system have to select the subnets that respond best to their specific input values. "This 'natural selection' concept differs

from other net theories in that it assumes the brain is made up of different subnets, and that, during learning, only those producing the
desired response will be selected."[75]

There is a feedback effect of modelling from the biological to the
artificial realm and back. Returning the compliment to the brain,
neural-network-based computers are used at the NASA Ames research
centre to "visualize the connectivity of real nervous systems and to
simulate nervous system behavior."[76] Ben Passarelli adds "using
their methods, scientists can now interact with the microscopic
world of neurons and test their theories and ideas about principles at
work in living systems." In the rapid exchange between the biological and artificial network models, we can see that the gap between
technology and psychology is narrowing.

NEURAL NETWORKS
AND EXPERT SYSTEMS

As explained earlier, computers can process in two modes, analogue
or digital. The kind of computer used to build "Expert Systems,"
presently the most common artificial intelligence technology, is
founded on digital operations, which are performed bit-by-bit.[77]
An expert system is a hierarchical set of data ruled by logical routines. It's used commercially to help doctors diagnose from sets of
systems or to help engineers realize set plans. The other kind of
computer technology, favoured and promoted by neural networks,
is founded on analogue operations performed interactively; that is,
by making and laying new patterns over previous patterns, checking
them and running over them again and again until a satisfactory
solution is reached.

TIME-BASED VERSUS
SPACE-BASED PROCESSING

It is not an oversimplification to propose that analogue and digital modes fit the distinctions between left and right brain modalities. Thus, analogue and digital processing systems could be considered as reflections of the basic biological or neuro-physiological processes we observed in Chapter 1. In them, you can recognize the different principles of the left and the right hemispheres of the brain: digital processing associated with time-based, analytic processing in the left hemisphere; analogue, with space-based holistic processing in the right hemisphere.[78] In technical applications, analogue and digital processing find their best expression in neural networks and expert systems. Their relation to the notion of a "mindset" is that analogue and digital are also the two basic program modes of mindsets influenced by computerization. The rivalry between the two is strong enough to engender discord. There can even be instances of downright hostility between these otherwise complementary mindsets.

Brody observes that "within artificial intelligence community, neural networks and expert systems sit on opposite sides of an almost ideological barrier."[79] I have witnessed heated debates between people who opted for IBM's MS/DOS system rather than Apple's WIMP technology and vice versa. Sometimes, people identify so closely with their training that they simply cannot see beyond it. The upshot, however, is that they tend to become caricatures of the system.

People who see red when they hear about the other side of the processing world are those who confuse mutual exclusion with incompatibility. I cannot be myself and my wife at the same time, but that does not imply that we are incompatible. That is the point. I tend to say analogue *and* digital rather than analogue *or* digital, because even though they are mutually exclusive, they should never be deemed to be incompatible. A measure of both is indispensable for any complex information processing. In that light, it may be instructive to compare their characteristics.

Comparison between expert systems and neural networks

Expert Systems	Neural Networks
linear	non-linear
vertical/hierarchical	lateral/mosaic
static	dynamic
digital	analogue
serial	parallel
specialist	generalist
computational models	neurobiological models
memory, number crunching, cognition	sensory projection
sequence analysis	pattern recognition
rule-based (needs rules)	example-based (finds rules)
domain specific	domain free
needs frequent updating	can update itself (adaptive)
not fault tolerant	fault tolerant
needs a human expert	needs a database
rigid logic	"fuzzy" logic
routine-based protocols	open-ended skills

It is worth expanding upon the last point. Because of the flexible learning patterns of neural networks, whether biological or technological, it's possible to train them for more than one type of activity. In other words, neural-network based computers can acquire cumulative skills, with the kind of necessary flexibility to relate to different occurrences. This is quite impossible for standard digital computers. Moreover, there are quite a few methods available to modify the response of neural networks. Each one confers a different set of skills to the system.[80]

APPLICATIONS

A few years ago, a rather entertaining scandal involving exaggerated claims about electro-chemical sensors in an aborted sale of "sniffer planes," supposedly able to detect oil fields, water reserves, pollution levels and nuclear silos. As it turned out, none of the claims could be substantiated and sales to a major European government were called off, to the great enjoyment of the media. At the time the claims did seem hard to swallow, but many stunning feats performed by today's neural networks do justify the faith of risk-taking executives selling today's sensory technology.

With over a hundred applications being developed in less than five years, some of which are listed below, we are certainly on the verge of a new cultural shift. There is even an experiment running at Stanford where a neural network is learning to drive a simulated forklift truck on an ever more complicated track, making its own decisions en route. The principal categories I have devised to group some of the more impressive feats of technological neural networks are:

- sensory modes ("eyes and ears")
- character recognition: sorting handwritten zip codes, vetting signatures, improving Optical Character Recognition (OCR) reading Japanese Kanji
- speech recognition
- smart weaponry (e.g., guiding missiles by matching the actual paths of their flight to an electronically mapped territory)
- trend predictions, diagnoses and prognoses (e.g., quickly spotting the fraudulent use of credit cards by analyzing sudden unusual buying patterns)
- chemical and molecular analysis
- matching picking and sorting tasks (e.g., helping robots to pick ripe produce and leaving immature fruit, or checking for faults in engines by listening for unusual sounds)
- vast improvement in radar and sonar technology (e.g., sensing rock formations in oil fields or improving sonar signal returns from ocean floors)
- noise cancellation in telecommunication systems
- banking operations (analyzing risks in loan and mortgage decisions)
- automated translation

A NOSE FOR BUSINESS

The extensions of sensory modalities are particularly impressive not only because neural networks give a new kind of wilfulness to video-audio devices, but especially because they may introduce yet another technological extension of our senses by adding smell and, possibly, taste. John Naisbitt reports that:

> Isao Karube, of the Tokyo Institute of Technology, has developed a "freshness chip," a device constituting entirely of artificially engineered proteins and organic polymers that will be built into packets of fish sold in supermarkets. When a fish begins to decay, it produces aromatic chemicals that the freshness chip detects long before it would be apparent to the average nose. When a patch on the fish changes color, customers (and management) know the fish's best days are over."[81]

Naisbitt adds that freshness chips for other foods will follow and that an artificial nose is expected "within the decade." Had he paid attention to neural networks, Naisbitt might be persuaded to agree that the artificial nose is already here in the form of computer-assisted airport luggage control, or in various neural networks used for spot checks by chemical engineers. The fact is, however, that neural networks are so versatile and apply to so many multi-sensory functions that they are better identified with "common sense" than with one particular sense or another. Thanks to neural networks, our visual, tactile, auditory and olfactory extensions are no longer passive conduits; they are becoming searching prostheses soon to be endowed with intentions and powers of decision. This will obviously mean upgrading our standard psychology.

ELECTRONIC WISDOM

Social critics of TV, video games and computers often complain about "info-glut," by which they mean that we receive too much information in too little time. People who complain about information overload are often print-dominated specialists, caught out by the flow of electronic information. The committed alphabetic mindset works like a hard-wired digital computer: it can only handle one subject at a time appearing in only one medium at a time. I have heard victims of such a constraining technology complain than they felt like frightfully slow computers.

The problem is that people completely underestimate their brains. That is probably because they make the wrong comparison with computers—or with the wrong kind of computers. They think that our brains are not fast enough. And of course, that is true, at least in comparison with digital computers. But, our brains do not need to be fast, it is enough that they be clever, that is, extremely well-wired and connected. In reality, our natural information processing capacities are much larger than we acknowledge. As McLuhan observed, "Information overload leads to pattern-recognition." That is precisely what neural networks are designed to do. Sooner or later, they'll be applied to verbal information gathering and sorting. One day they may even be taught to read your paper for you and pick out what you need to know, or select the TV shows you can't afford to miss. Will we ever see the day of "neural couch potatoes"?

CHAPTER FOURTEEN

THE SKIN OF CULTURE

DESIGNING
NEW TECHNOLOGIES

I N KEEPING with the general idea that technologies generate techno-cultural fields, it is interesting to examine whether such currents also affect industrial design. As one of the most visible afterimages of technology, design lends us a means of identifying patterns in the maze of cultural change. Production values may also offer us a deep insight into cultural biases and prejudices. The prime example is Japan, not only because of the country's special place in the world economy, but also because few other cultures reveal in their products so clear an indication about what conditions their senses. As economies globalize, it will become essential to know about such things—things Edward Hall has been exploring ever since he wrote *The Silent Language*, a ground-breaking study of cultural relativity.[82]

DESIGN:
THE SKIN OF CULTURE

It seems that design is technology's public relations, glamorizing its products and sharpening its image in the marketplace. The particular design that envelops a technology, say the flattened cone shape and sleek elongation of the French TGV high-speed train, represents it and promotes it, whether directly or subliminally. However, design is more than an afterthought, bolted onto industrial production to facilitate marketing. There is clearly more to design than containment and seduction. In a very large sense, design plays a metaphorical role, translating functional benefits into sensory and cognitive modalities. Design finds its shape and its place as a kind of overtone, as an echo of technology. Design often echoes the specific character of technology and corresponds to its basic pulse. Being the visible, audible or textural outer shape of cultural artifacts, design emerges as what can be called the "skin of culture." Some examples of technological overtones in design are:

- Raymond Loewy's streamlining of modes of transportation that extended to a whole range of products including refrigerators, toasters and, of course, the classic Coca-Cola bottle design.
- Jazz, rock and disco musical styles that followed, respectively, radio, television and computers, to say nothing about direct techno-magnetic field shopping via Muzak.
- Dieter Rams' streamlined functionalism for the BrAun line that influenced not only other nations' design practices but typified BrAun products as the German line par excellence.
- French nouvelle cuisine that extended the Bauhaus effect to the texture and freshness of foodstuff.

Because, at any given period, design affects more than a single object or product line, it brings out what one could call the "harmonics" of culture. Each technology produces harmonic overtones in sound, taste, smell, colour and form. Design, of course, can express itself at many levels and in many metaphorical modes. Some examples of these are:

- sensory modes (colour, shapes, tastes, textures): for example, the Impressionists' response to photography, television's psychedelia or the pretend rejection of formal grids in post-modern design of materials and textures;

- cognitive modes: the Hula hoop was a cognitive response to the matricial embrace of television while the Rubik cube was the image of the expression of rotational cognitive operations with early CAD-CAM;
- organizational mode: One fascinating effect of television on organizational design modes was identified by William S. Kowinski: "The mall is a visual experience. It's TV that you walk around in. People-watching is what people do in the mall when they aren't looking for something to buy. The images they see in the mall are from television; and how they see and accept these images has been conditioned by watching television."[83]

The development and the patterns of techno-cultural fields depend upon such harmonics; technologies are like musical instruments played by the whole culture over a period of time. Overtones are picked up, amplified and distributed by the industry.

THE HARMONICS OF TECHNOLOGY IN DESIGN

Design gives unity to a period. Antiques are dated and collected on the basis of the design school to which they belong. Similarly, modern artifacts can be related by their design. Psychedelics and Andy Warhol characterized the sixties. The style, shapes and colours of McDonald's outlets and the loose features of the Sesame Street muppets belong in the same category—as artifacts of TV's recent mass culture. There is often a cult cartoon character shared equally by packaged goods, a children's TV show and gasoline ads. On the other hand, discreet high-tech styles uniformly replaced brash art during the eighties. This is surely a psychological side-effect of the computerized techno-cultural field. After all, real "high technology" hardly ever escapes the lab or the military base. Only the ubiquitous presence of microchips in the most mundane appliances could have inspired our craving for high-tech styles and fashions.

Even unintentional design appears among random forms and motifs. Unplanned design quite spontaneously reflects the cultural origins of its products. It is interesting for example, to track multicultural influences on the outskirts of American and Canadian cities. You can always spot the Chinese building even before you find the first ideogram, simply by noticing that the ratio of horizontal to vertical lines in windows is not the standard western 3 to 4, but 4 to 5.

But design, as the word implies quite forcefully, is planned. Design, as I understand it, is a modulation of the relationship between the human body and the environment as it is modified by technology. Technology comes out of the human body and design makes sense of it. The only serious difference between body and mind, in my opinion, is that the mind is conscious. In every other way, mind and body are so intermingled that it is pointless to separate them, even in theory. Still, to a degree, the mind has to become conscious of the changes in the total ecology of self. Since this is not always easy, this is where design comes in. By observing the specific values of design, the mind learns to interpret the postures of our extended bodies. Whether you look at the nose of the TGV, or at the tiny but powerful earphones of Sony's Walkman, it's the design that brings their functional and sensory effects to your attention. It is design that helps us to integrate the speed and the power of the bullet train within our muscular system. It is design that makes our nervous system accept the intimate, cyborgian coupling of the headphones.

HOW DESIGN RESPONDS TO TECHNOLOGICAL PRESSURE

Design may reflect creative aggression and often elicits aggression from consumers before they become acclimatized. Every new musi-

cal genre raises the same level of hostility from those who were committed to the previous one. New styles are derided before they're
adopted by the very same people. Indeed, far from condemning the
tastes and forms that have eventually saturated a culture—pop culture in the seventies or post-modernism in the eighties—critics
ought to recognize that there lie the most successful and effective
designs, in so far as they have succeeded in gaining mass acceptance.

"WHEN YOUR INSIDE'S OUT AND YOUR OUTSIDE'S IN"

As extensions of our inner selves, electronic technologies bring into
the open objects and products that emulate our internal environments. This has an interesting impact on design. At the height of the
TV era, the trend of personal psychology was to "let it all hang out."
After decades of post-war repression, expressed in the sleek lines of
Modernist architecture and design, people began to recover their
libidos—wanted to open up and show everything. A good example
of how this was translated, even into the conservative world of architecture, is the arresting Pompidou Centre in Paris. Though unat-
tractive to some, it is the most fascinating satire of the modernist
steel-and-glass style ever made. All the features that normally go
inside a building are on the outside, plumbing, wiring, heating
ducts, the lot.

In the late sixties and early seventies, sculptors sponsored by corporations would construct huge structures of rusting steel outside
clean-cut, streamlined plants. In a wry humorous fashion, these
artists were pointing out that the days of the mechanical era were
over. At least, that is what they thought. In fact, they were reacting
to television, which was bringing out all our inner functions and
pouring them out into the open. But today, things have changed
again: the silent efficiency of instant computer communication is
turning the old hardware into software and bringing functions so
deeply inside that you can't see them any more.

INTERNALIZING

After the first flush of fascination with a new technology, especially one just handed down from the professional to the domestic market, internalization is much in evidence. Admittedly, a few people still proudly show you their fitted furniture, or the buttons on the ghetto blaster, or the cellphone in their car. This may be a necessary stage of externalization that each technology must go through to penetrate a culture, a process that takes some technologies longer than others. Computers, though, are already on the brink of disappearing into the woodwork. Japanese designers are using more and more internal computerized functions to explore the featureless look: geometrical steel and plastic boxes responding to gesture and proximity-command without revealing so much as an on-off button.

EXPLOSION

The art world is very sensitive to the shrapnel of cultures that have exploded. For example, the development of the telegraph and the telephone, which shrunk space and time, blew apart the gentle pace of colonial times. Academic art and bourgeois furnishings were smashed to bits in the minds of the artists and writers who inspired Futurism in Italy and later Dada and Surrealism in France. Dada announced the blow-up by deriding conventions and Surrealism picked up the pieces to put them into a new and amusingly irrational order.

There is a marvellously structural example of this in Salvador Dali's copy of a Madonna by Raphael, painted as if it were subjected to an explosion within. The power of this work comes from the violent contrast between the softness of the Raphaelian image and the sharpness of the shards. At the same time, there is a reassuring, mystical quality to the painting, as if the artist's formidable sense of humour came from absolute confidence in a fundamental order of things. These parodies of cultures in disorder broke up the stuffy bourgeois order of the nineteenth-century realists. The introduction of television heralded the Theatre of the Absurd, which suggested that our rationalistic psychology and our perspectivist mindset were no longer attuned to the realities of our new techno-cultural field.

IMPLOSION

Computers, by accelerating the pace of our television culture, have generated the Post-Modernist implosion. The typical Post-Modern building quotes previous eras and styles. It may appear as a jumble of incompatible features, as if it had been subjected to a rapid implosion after the explosion of the sixties and seventies. Or as if fragments of past cultures have suddenly landed to decorate facades and furniture. Whenever there is this kind of blow-up followed by recovery, parody, humour and irony are dominant.

One such amusing architectural statement can be found in one of the Steinberg Department stores in Arizona. It derides stark and featureless modernist shapes by having one of the building's lower corners literally break off for the main entrance. You can even see the jagged edges at the point of breaking. Post-Modernist style is an example of humour being fully and elegantly integrated in the solemn business of architecture. The freedom of style in Post-Modernism expresses a human need to recover scale in an increasingly technological environment. By contrast, Modernism sprang from a world in which people did not feel threatened by technology. Mies Van Der Rohe was putting large scale vertical monoliths in horizontal urban areas still working to the scale imposed by Haussmann in nineteenth-century Paris.

COMPUTER-ASSISTED DESIGN

Computer systems afford instant access to vast amounts of information about the design and artifacts of previous cultures. As an architect you can call up on your screen just about any period or style in stark detail. Use a professional 3-D simulation package and you can watch it evolve or view it from any angle. Through computer-assisted design, instant simulations show how a building might look with ornamental as well as structural changes. This kind of power encourages architects and designers to explore previous eras and re-integrate them into a sort of extended present. The technological collective memory provides the means for endless explorations in several levels of time. A good definition of time accelerated by computer is that the past becomes integrated in a huge extended present.

THE ENCOUNTER OF TECHNO-CULTURAL FIELDS WITH JAPANESE CULTURE

When Commodore Perry gave a steam locomotive to the Shogun Ieyasu in 1854 to celebrate the official opening of U.S.-Japanese trade, the Shogun sent his court artist to paint it, as he could not come to see it in person. The Japanese artist found it so difficult to represent the new object that he added a postscript for the Shogun's benefit. "I fear I have made many errors in this sketch."[84] We have tendency to find quaint or amusing such occurrences at the cross-roads of cultures, but it should not obscure the reality that, when a new technology is introduced, it wages an undeclared war upon the existing culture.

To a culture whose doors had been shut to outside influences for several centuries, the Industrial Revolution came with an aggressive and centralizing force. "The train was feverishly built to connect all parts of Japan, not only as a symbol of progress and a unifier of eco-nomics, but as a part of the militarization of Japan."[85] Unlike West-ern industrialists, the Japanese favoured building railways over roadways. Fosco Moraini explains that, for a very long time, the Japanese people resisted buying private cars. "A car implies individu-alism, independence, making sudden decisions, all things which go against the grain of the Japanese mentality. In a country of such close social texture, individual initiative is fundamentally suspect."[86] Today, however, cars are a major export and congest Japanese cities. A survey in Osaka, in 1964, noted that there had been 4,524 traffic jams at least a half-mile in length and lasting more than 30 minutes resulting in 5,508 hours of traffic stoppage.[87]

MOULTING AS A RESPONSE TO TECHNOLOGICAL ACCELERATION

In a country such as Japan, being invaded by successive waves of techno-cultural fields, it takes an exceptionally gifted people to maintain a balance between tradition and innovation. This balance is all but lost in many other countries that have been subjected to technological acceleration. The Japanese went through the traumas of mass industrialization in much the same way as Western nations, only very much faster. The speed of adaptation has never let up. Now it's still accelerating, with the shift from a mechanical, hardware-based industry to the electronic software economy. This means that the Japanese have had to "learn on the job" in order to integrate the new into the old.

When submitted to pressures of large-scale social change, minority cultures, depending upon the strength of their identity, will respond with emerging patterns of assimilation, integration, alienation or aggression. Having released a formidable burst of aggression in the Second World War, the Japanese have found a new response: moulting. By moulting, you change the appearance of culture but not its content. It is on the surface of their culture, not in its core, that the Japanese drama of adaptation is played.

Popular design can provide clues as to how a culture is reacting to the onslaught of technology. Godzilla, a typically Japanese invention, could be an apt, albeit unconscious, metaphor for the effect of the automobile on the Japanese city. Godzilla is the ultimate traffic jam: antediluvian (obsolete), heavy (unsubtle), stupid (unthinking), slow-moving (urban paralysis at rush hour) and stinking (spewing forth carbon monoxide). There is, of course, a fusion of myths in this new incarnation of the old Chinese dragon theme. If the special fondness of the Japanese for Godzilla movies is the response of Japan's helplessness to being invaded by industry, then Transformers demonstrate a second stage, one where the "enemy" is conquered by the best features of the Japanese national character.

Canadian sociologist Mark Segal reminds us that the Transformers that invaded the American toy market were actually bred upon Japanese ground.[88] Segal notes that like American popular folklore, the Japanese variety is obsessed with the fear of invasion by alien forces.*

The fantasy of alien persecution, despite any hard evidence to support it, is, of course, a kind of traumatic metaphor. It could be the psychological effect of the technologies attacking the culture. But we should observe that the Japanese variety is curiously more intimate than the standard "good-guys-versus-bad-guys" type. Indeed, transformers are creatures of design that are both organic and mechanical in turn. What could be a closer approximation of the uneasy adjustment of Japanese psychology to the cyborgian integration of man and machine? By comparison, westerners have been raped by their machines almost without noticing it. In essence, the western equivalent to the Japanese Transformer are *Bladerunner's* androids, mechanization taking an organic form; Transformers portray organic beings turning mechanical in self-defence.

Commenting on Segal's paper, Stephen Kline says:

> The Japanese science fiction tradition has become extremely popular because it vivifies on the screen a number of essentially Japanese cultural traits, among which are fear of invasion and

---

* It is interesting to note that three among the most powerful nations of the world, namely the United States, Russia and Japan, nations that presumably have the least to fear from outside aggression, are also those that seem to favour the most aggressive mythologies in their popular media. The aggression could be no more, no less than a projection of the culture's fear of itself and of its own transformation.

encroachment from aliens, componentialization, hierarchical social structure, selfless dedication to the group, stoicism in the face of danger, a need to perform at the peak of one's personal capacity, and a Japanese model of group interdependence and decision-making . . . in the American toy market the gobots and autobots indicate other societies' relationships to modern technology, behind which is a message about their relationship to Western ways.[89]

However, the strategy of transforming adopted by the Japanese is the opposite of a mutation, because the core elements of the culture are not affected. It is a moulting. The Japanese put on technology like a new set of clothes. Instead of letting themselves be run over (the Godzilla syndrome), the Japanese find it easier to put on their cars, to wear them. Transformers have been a kind of boil on the skin of their cultural moulting.

TRANSFORMERS AS THE POPULAR IMAGE OF "MECHATRONIC"

By the unique design of their toys and the narratives attached to them, the Japanese have fashioned a mythological response that can be easily generalized in their culture. Comments Kline: "At the end of each story, when the invaders must once again be defeated, the components of the combat team reassemble into a giant robot warrior that battles with the alien machine. The battle is won through the co-operation and dedication of the team against individualist mechanical gain."[90] Thus the most interesting reading of the Transformers metaphor reveals Transformers as the symbolic totems of the new breed of Japanese entrepreneurs, the new samurais, waging war by industrial instead of military means.

If the modular integration of the various parts of the single megarobot tells us something abut the Japanese character, the marriage of mechanical and electronic technologies in the Transformer itself tells the story of Japanese industry. Indeed, the sharp, hard edges and busy lines of the toys seem to betray the fact that the Japanese industry has neither fully absorbed nor divested itself of its mechanical heritage. There is something clumsy about Transformers, like an uneasy, incomplete incarnation. The development of Transformers dates from the time the industry went overboard for what the Japanese call mechatronics.

> Old hat now, mechatronics was one of those technological feats that go beyond mere innovation. As its name implies, it fused ideas from the greasy world of machinery with notions drawn from electronics. The products it bequeathed range from the lowly digital watch to the modern NC (numerically-controlled) machine tool.[91]

However, the impact of electronics on culture in Japan may be very different from the impact of mechanization. It may soon have a healing effect on the social and cultural wounds opened up by industrialization. In fact, there is a possibility that the Japanese have developed a greater familiarity with electronic technologies precisely because electricity is closer to their cultural psychology. Electricity enables us to modulate the intervals of space, something Japanese learn to do from birth simply by observing their traditions. On the other hand, what the Japanese might perceive as an opportunity to reaffirm their identity could one day be interpreted by westerners as a threat, precisely because the latter have developed such a completely different sense of space.

THE MYTH OF "NEUTRAL" SPACE

Our architecture since the Renaissance clearly shows that we have tended to consider space as something that can be divided neatly into public and private property. Space, in and of itself, used to be considered neutral in a western perspectivist mindset. The traditional western notion of the environment is that it is an empty stage for human and elemental activities. Until the early part of the twentieth century, westerners assumed that the air was empty and by no means sacred. Under the protection of their private individual skins, they tended to feel immune to the consequences of their own inventions.

But today's space is invaded by electronic, molecular and viral communication networks. The air is not empty anymore. That is why westerners are becoming so conscious of pollution and the environment. 'Pollution' comes from the Latin *pulvis* which means powder. Indeed, most people imagine pollution as fine particles of unidentified foreign substances. However, pollution is both a physical and a psychological reality. We hear more about industrial pollution than about electronic pollution. That is because as we emerge into a new era we tend to consider the previous one as dirty. Now, the dust is from the abrasion of different materials, technologies or, at the psychological level, ideologies. As a consequence, we feel threatened on many levels. Our health, privacy and autonomy as individuals are threatened by chemical, molecular, physical, industrial and psychological agents. The myth of pollution is the metaphor of the discovery by the West that space is alive and can therefore be killed.

M A

The Japanese, on the other hand, have never taken to the western notion of neutral space. In traditional Japanese culture, space is not neutral and has never been so. For the Japanese, space is a continuous flow, alive with interactions and ruled by a precise sense of timing and pacing. The name for that is *ma*. Ma is the Japanese word for space or "space-time," but it does not correspond to our idea of space. The main difference is that when we say space we imply room or empty areas. To the Japanese, ma connotes the complex network of relationships between people and objects. A French expert on Japan, Michel Random says

> In Japan, everything depends on ma: the martial arts as well as architecture, music or the plain art of living. Aesthetics, proportions, garden design, all belong to networks of meanings which are related to each other through ma. Even business people in Japan obey the laws of ma when they approach each other; the idea is to sense how your partner judges things. Ma will then dictate the hierarchy of choices, the priorities of investments, the right time and the proper pace in the organization of the enterprise, and shape the exact perception of people and situations. In a word, ma is perceived behind everything as an undefinable musical chord, a sense of the precise interval eliciting the fullest and finest resonance.[92]

The Japanese have a keen awareness of the interval. Japanese design reveals an awareness of the space between things rather than a fixation on the object, for example flower arrangement, gardening or hierarchical human interactions. It is therefore not surprising that Japanese industries today show such a keen interest in design. In a way, electricity and airwaves can give us a much better idea about how the Japanese understand space than our own idea of space.

PSYCHOTECHNOLOGICAL MA

Our most recent electronic technologies invite East to meet West in a totally new way: everybody will be related at different levels in a kind of electronic ma. As we develop closer and closer interfaces between our mind and our technologies, we can expect very soon to "think" on-line. The externalization of these functions may provoke a situation where machines become more and more autonomous. But man-machine interactions also fill the so-called objective world with thick networks of activities. This is the psychotechnological ma, a world of electronic intervals in constant activity and reverberations. Design will quickly progress from an essentially reactive to a gradually more proactive stage. New technologies should become the object of design, rather than being at the source of design. Design will find more rewarding fields in exploring and creating patterns of interfacing than in the production of objects.

This is an area where Japanese designers and engineers should excel. Indeed the source of inspiration for design modalities in the near future will not be limited to traditional notions of beauty and efficiency, but will include the recovery of our most ancient need for wisdom. This is because of the very excess of our powers. When you can do anything and everything, the next step must be to find out who you really are and what you really want. The present is too busy to give us much information on that. So we may soon have to replace the mythology of progress for progress' sake by a return to the Golden Ages of the world's cultures.

In that sense, the Japanese concept of ma has much to offer modern Japan and the modern world generally. Ma is the quintessence of a certain aspect of the global human civilization. By understanding and especially by perceiving ma, designers and planners could begin to recover the human dimensions and proportions now lost in the technological invasion. The main role of the artist or the designer in the context of unlimited power and access is to probe history, natural and social—to cull guidelines from mankind's more successful experiments in living.

CHAPTER FIFTEEN

VOLCANIC ART

I N TIMES of unrest and social turmoil, art deals with values. In quieter times, art can afford to contribute to ornamentation and order. In times of violent psychic upheavals like our own, art is not an escape, not a way out of confusion and incertitude, but a way in, a peephole into the churning of collective consciousness, the magma of reality in the making. Eagerly, we search for meaning. Our values have been shaken by a rapid succession of ideological bankruptcies: by communism, Nazism, existentialism, Marxism, socialism, capitalism, consumerism, Freudism, new leftism, Thatcherism, Reaganism, hippies and yuppies. The images of men and women, our own self-images, television myths, the thirst for balance and order—all these notions float in a magma of drives, desires, frustrations, hopes, disappointments and broken promises. Why are we in such a psychological mess in times of such technological progress? And a second, just as critical question: Why are we still incapable of sharing our resources in times of such comprehensive and hemispheric abundance?

Because much of our life and culture depends on technology, it may be useful to reassess the relationship between art and culture and technology. My volcanic metaphor of art is based on the—admittedly Jungian—idea that art, as a product of collective unconsciousness, erupts at the surface of consciousness when the crust of reality is too weak to support the status quo. The first question is why does the so-called crust of reality become weak? Because, fundamentally, reality is technology-dependent, it changes every time new technologies invade it. A worldview based on print is challenged and weakened by the appearance of television, just as a worldview based on broadcast television is deeply threatened by computer networks. Reality is a form of consensus supported not only by the goodwill and the language of the communities that share it, but also framed and maintained by the principal medium of communication used by that culture. Art erupts when a new technology challenges the status quo.

Indeed, technologies invade reality with little or no conscious resistance on the part of those who readily adopt them. Technological drives and market promises, as well as rampant techno-fetishism, numb the buying public who remain psychologically bound to past images of themselves and of the world. Current artists are the hot and conscious tips of a large somnambulistic public iceberg. They question the effects of the latest technologies such as computers, interactive systems, multimedia, virtual reality and any other device on the marketable horizon, not in a naïvely political way, but at a deeper psycho-sensorial level. Who are we? What are these machines doing to us? What reflections do they give of ourselves? How are they transforming our own images of who we still think we are? The first products of such earnest questions encounter stiff disapproval and resistance from the art establishment as well as from the gallery-going public.

A romantic, idealized view would proffer a volcanic theory as follows: the art work breaks through the crust of weakened reality consensus like a threat. Sparks and fireworks generate much opposition from the establishment. Fierce opposition to innovation is the standard response of any establishment, whether political, religious, economic or scientific. Fear and loathing greeted the works of Courbet and Manet and the early films of Resnais; and the last *Dokumenta* international exhibition in Kassel, Germany made a joke of any representation of technology in art. The new reality, a new consciousness in ebullition, still pouring out of the volcanic mouth, travels down the slopes of the mountain, slowing down and cooling off on its way. The further from the top, the cooler and darker it is, until it reaches the point of sedimentation. The last stage is memory, the museum, the institution. The sediment is just as important as the spark, if we want coherence and meaning in culture. The issue is not to brand and label the product, but to observe the process of art in response to technology.

This view is romantic and idealized because in the new globalized mass multiculture, the work of art is drowned in the din of mass media and popular culture. But, precisely because they are globalized by instant communications, the artworld from Tokyo to Paris to Amsterdam to Glasgow to Québec City or Johannesberg and Wichita, Kansas, is in touch instantly with what goes on. In the world's nervous system, art works to best effects in small doses.

Art is born out of technology. It is the counterforce that balances the disruptive effects of new technologies in culture. Art is the metaphorical side of the very technology it uses and criticizes. For example, while print was invented to represent and distribute information, theatre, novels and poetry, as well as perspectivist painting, sculpture and architecture were developed as metaphors of the human condition subjected to literacy. As westerners, we owe the structure of our consciousness to literacy and the stuff of our sensibility, the contents of our psychological make-up, to the works of Da Vinci, Shakespeare, Racine, Voltaire, Spinoza, Rembrandt, Vermeer, Dostoyevsky and scores of artists who have patiently built the walls of our private consciousnesses and decorated them.

In the much accelerated technological context of the present and the recent past, we must rely on art and popular culture to integrate our own contraptions: we accept automobiles, television and computers in our lives—not always uncritically—but often without observing that each one of these devices is going to make a large dent, not only in our wallets but also, more precisely, in our psyches. Each technological extension that we allow into our lives behaves as a kind of phantom limb, never quite integrated into our body or mind functions, but never really out of our psychological make-up either.

Take a look at an older home defaced by a monumental, add-on garage. It is the architectural image of our bloated consumer culture and also of our psychological build-up. To make room for one's car in one's home is to deface it. To allow that car into our lifeform, our total being, is to weigh it down, to load it with a service station, a landscape of asphalt and city suburbs with gasoline advertising and carbon dioxide.

If that is the kind of world we have to wear, so be it. But every now and then a work of art appears somewhere in the world, in the media, that raises the issue of our identity. Take, for example, Eugene Ionesco's play *Rhinoceros*. His thinly disguised metaphor of ordinary human beings turning into rhinoceroses has often been interpreted as yet another fable of fascism, a throw-back to earlier protests against human acceptance of an oppressive social order. However, chances are that, as it was performed in the early sixties, *Rhinoceros* was more likely a subconscious response to the rising fortunes of General Motors, Renault, Mercedes-Benz and British Leyland. Who would deny that we identify so much with our automobiles that we might as well wear them?

Art does not always succeed in redressing the lost balance, but it always tries to give shape and meaning to the culture thus disrupted. For example, Italian Futurism and Modernism in sculpture, architecture and painting in the late 1800s and early 1900s accompanied and supported the biases of the industrial revolution that had disrupted the slower rhythms of agrarian culture. The art of Marinetti, Boccioni, Léger and others attempted to give new, aggressive values based on the craft of Vulcan. This trend led to the First World War, a further and more radical effect of technological acceleration.

The issue of acceleration is paramount. In a stable culture, where technological turnover is slow, it is the state that supports and controls culture. The Golden Ages of Pericles in Greece and of the Sun King in France correspond to periods of techno-cultural stabilization during which there is the beginning of piecing together of social consciousness, communication infrastructures and state control. In our own time, technological revolutions happen too fast to reach a mature stage. When technological innovation accelerates, market forces take over. The task of collective harmonization and psycho-sensorial education is given to popular culture. Twentieth-century equivalents to Michelangelo are Rudolf Valentino and Madonna.

Moving at very high speeds, technology itself controls the marketplace and, hence, culture. There used to be a time when history was reality; today reality is in great danger of becoming history. Right now, Nintendo tunes the nervous systems of generations exposed more frequently to computers than to television screens. While they are playing, our kids are turned into hapless extensions of their Nintendos and Segas, as if they were complex, organic servomechanisms of crude joysticks and digital video cartoons. That's another image of our new selves growing up.

Technological art is entering the second phase of the volcanic process, pouring out of the volcano and cooling fast enough for people to approach it. It is a time of great expectations and hope for a better understanding of the complexities of a world suddenly made larger for individuals and smaller for collectivities. As people, we are searching for an expanded perception of ourselves, commensurate with the global reach of our technological phantom limbs. As a world multiculture, we are looking for patterns of integration beyond the strife of linguistic, ethnic, political, religious and economic differences. We need more, not fewer global metaphors to begin to recognize our planet not only as our home, but as our very body.

CHAPTER SIXTEEN

CYBORG ECOLOGIES

BIOMECHANICS

"The mind, once expanded to the dimensions of larger ideas, never returns to its original size."

– Oliver Wendell Holmes

CYBORG REALITY

IT IS ALREADY POSSIBLE to order machines to do simple jobs by thought alone. Eye and voice command interfaces are in development. The last boundary to the true biotechnical relationship between human and machine is the interface itself. This may not necessarily be desirable, but it should not obscure the fact that we have been entertaining quasi-bionic relationships with our inventions all along. Jean-Jacques Rousseau notwithstanding, there has never been such a thing as a "natural man."

The idea of a biotechnical being was popularized by Arnold Schwarzenegger in the *Terminator* films. Outwardly his body looked the same as yours or mine, but when his skin was damaged or ripped, you could see the wiring. *Bladerunner's* androids, on the other hand, were a lot more sophisticated: they were programmable genetic mutants, not just technological robots. The fact is, if you accept a large part of this book, you might have to conclude that we are all more or less programmable, if not genetic mutants. This shouldn't be cause for alarm, more, a call for precision in knowing who we are.

NATURE
VERSUS CULTURE

Today, our technologies are so versatile that they give us the power to re-design what we call "reality." With technologies managing our time, space and selves, the traditional balance has been tripped in favour of culture over nature. Our genetic code may want to tell us when to eat or sleep, but we keep trying to say something else—the prescriptive safeguards of our planet have been all but dismantled. That doesn't imply that we must immediately throw ourselves onto the environmentalist bandwagon. The solution is not in fingerwagging, but in adopting the new responsibilities towards planetary ecology that our new powers invest in us. Because these powers often ignore the conventional guidelines of nature, we now have to make choices within a multiplicity of possibilities. Today, we can do anything we want, so we first need to know what we want.

TECHNOPSYCHOLOGICAL
TRENDS

I would like to venture a few predictions, though I am ever mindful of McLuhan's recommendation, "To be a good prophet, never predict anything that hasn't already happened."[93] Here, then, are a few trends that might have escaped the attention of some, if not all, of the management gurus.

LOSS OF PSYCHOLOGICAL BOUNDARIES BETWEEN SELF AND ENVIRONMENT

With virtual realities upon us, we may find it increasingly difficult to distinguish between our "natural" selves and the electronic extensions. The problem arises from the electrical nature of both our biological and our technological environments. The Italian design historian Claudia Donà elegantly expresses how electricity has become the medium of biotechnical relationships between our bodies and our environment.

> The low voltage current flowing in a printed circuit functions in a manner akin to the bodily cell. The traces of an electronic circuit are taking on organic forms. Artificial memories are now tending to dispense with their mechanical supports to establish themselves as solid concentrations of information: and with the elimination of the interface, the user's relationship to the microprocessor has also taken on a "natural" quality.[94]

Donà also suggests the emergence of a new kind of human, searching for global bearings. "As Telematic Nomads, we have been freed from the constraints of a historical and 'unique' coincidence between 'place' and 'time,' and can realize in its stead the power of being everywhere while remaining in one place."[95] This realization brings with it the responsibility of expanding our psychological selves beyond the limits of the skin and the body.

POINT-OF-BEING VERSUS POINT-OF-VIEW

"Wearing mankind as our skin," as McLuhan proposed,[96] may soon become not an option but an eco-psychological necessity. One way to go about this is to let go of our unidimensional points-of-view and recognize that they are quickly being overtaken by the new perception of our "point-of-being." The real question is, where do we fit in, as individuals, in this sudden expansion of consciousness that is shrinking the planet?

The idea of a point-of-being enables us to keep track of ourselves when our technologically extended senses are operating all over the planet. It is our only physical reference point in the total surround of our electronic projections. The physical sensation of being somewhere specific is a tactile experience, not a visual one. It is environmental, not frontal. It is comprehensive, not exclusive. My point-of-being, instead of distancing me from reality like a point-of-view, becomes my point of entry into sharing the world.

As we enter new time scales, ranging from nanoseconds to millennia, and reach from the subatomic to the planetary system, the environment ceases to relate to the scale of the human body. We are yanked out of the humanist tradition altogether. Renaissance man is no longer the model. Once you realize that your self is no longer separated from the environment, you will suddenly become a much larger person.

INSIDE/OUTSIDE; MAINLINING ELECTRICITY

Once the traditional boundaries separating self from environment begin to blur, there begins a cross-flow within and without the body. As we start to "mainline" electricity, we can entertain "inside/outside" notions such as those of the Greeks, who believed that they "breathed in" their thoughts and perceptions. This trend encourages the observation that the environment itself is breathed in, becoming an object of perception and evaluation in its own terms. In keeping with this metaphor, an emerging image of a human is of one breathing in complex information and breathing out transformed materials. A further reason to reassess our relationship to the environment is that there are now alternative environments that appear on our screens as virtual realities.

A NEW SENSIBILITY

Why is it that, after decades of tobacco, alcohol and dietary abuse, we are suddenly obsessed with fitness? Today, people are stopping smoking en masse. Executives are out in shorts, running off the effects of the comfortable office, the automobile and the business lunch. Why this sudden change of mood, which is making the boards of certain "unhealthy" industries nervous?

By highlighting our nervous systems, the Electronic Age has made us more sensitive to the danger of losing our bodies. Smoking was once meant, like alcohol, to separate our minds from our bodies. Now that communications are taking over, we want more, rather than less contact with ourselves. By going straight to the nervous system, electrical technology is emulating our sensory modes. Television in the sixties injected massive amounts of sensory experience and provoked an orgy of sensory rediscovery. With the advent of computers, that has been turned around into a feeling for our organic integrity. We are not yet fully ecological, but we have become much more demanding about the management of our environment. The environment has ceased to be a neutral container for our activities. It is made of information, it is becoming "intelligent" and, via the media, everything is coming out into the open.

CHAPTER SEVENTEEN

COLLECTIVE
INTELLIGENCE

THE RISE OF THE INTERNET
AND THE GLOBAL VILLAGE

Electric speed tends to abolish time and space in human awareness. There is no delay in the effect of one event upon another. The electric extension of the nervous system creates the unified field of organically interrelated structures that we call the present Age of Information.

– Marshall McLuhan[97]

RES PUBLICA

R*ES PUBLICA*, the 'public thing,' was the Romans' idea of how to organize a society of equals. It was western democracy's earliest concept of "public domain." At the time no one coined the corollary expression *res privata*, the "private thing," but the exercise of the right to privacy depends absolutely on a recognition of the public domain. It is only within the limits of what is public that you can claim privacy. This distinction is very clear. Democracy is based on it.

Electricity has accelerated the public realm, via TV, as well as the private realm, via computers and computer networks. However, with the convergence of TV and computers within the confines of wired and cellular networks, the distinction between public and private realms is beginning to blur.

The space of the Internet is not neutral, it has no border, it is not stable nor is it unified. It is organic. Its motion is perpetual and it behaves like a self-organizing system. Our obsolescent political notions are going to be thoroughly trashed by it.

THE GLOBAL VILLAGE IN THE NEO-NATIONALIST ERA

The image of a "global village," introduced by Marshall McLuhan, seems to fly in the face of the increasing regionalism, separatism and local strife that appears daily on our television screens. Critics have begun to condemn McLuhan's metaphor, but in their zeal they have over-literalized his global village concept. Originally it was a generalization meant to give the complex theatre of international telecommunications a handle. Just as a city becomes an entity on the basis of place, the global village was the first name given to the Earth as a single telecommunicative community. What irks contemporary critics is their association of a village with rural quietude, and, comparing this with daily evidence of the rise of neo-nationalism, they scoff at any suggestion that the Earth is being successful at striving for equilibrium.

One of the more valuable implications of the global village metaphor is the notion of scale. There is less room to move in a village than in a city. Telecommunications impose a forced association; an implosive—and potentially explosive—situation has been thrust upon us. Human communities living at different speeds, with hugely different levels of social expertise, are thrown upon each other without any warning or mediation. There are no protocols to prepare us for these pell-mell confrontations, no training in social or collective behaviour. The more globally conscious we become, the more aware and protective we find ourselves about our local identities, hence the paradox of the global village. The hyper-local is the necessary complement to the hyper-global.

The notion of the global village arose in the midst of the era of television, when analogue images dominated public consciousness. Though the culture had been global for some time, it was possible for McLuhan to coin the expression "global village" because television gave us a sense of the different nations on the Earth. We were all villagers on the same planet. Of course, we still are, even if we don't always get along.

GLOBAL CONSCIOUSNESS

Television was responsible for the dominance of spatial relations in our imagination. Every television network more or less connects its representation of reality with any other network, particularly when both are involved in reporting news, sports or any "live" event. This is what makes the world a village where everybody knows everybody else or, at the very least, where everybody agrees more or less reluctantly that everybody else shares the same space. Today the very idea of that space is being challenged by a completely new kind of conscious experience, the like of which mankind had never really known before, and for which we do not yet have a psychological vocabulary.

Indeed, the fundamental issue of globalization is that of consciousness. While social critics such as Hans Magnus Enzensberger, Jurgen Habermas, Jean Baudrillard and many others have correctly recognized consciousness as a new industrial product, their inherently political approach has narrowed their focus, away from the more comprehensive development now underway. For the first time in world history, we are accelerating towards a new level of consciousness that is both collective and private at once . There are at least three features of the present trend towards globalization that invite psychological (rather than exclusively political) considerations: transparency, instantaneity and intelligent environments.

TRANSPARENCY

Global transparency arises from instant news distribution and world access via media. It may be somewhat of an illusion, but it is a very powerful one because it proposes the whole world as a field for consciousness, encompassing not only one's own consciousness, but that of larger social entities as well. And to those who are still claiming that telecommunications are the latest form of colonization, I would like to suggest that the colonizers are always the first victims of the colonizing technology, usually because they remain resolutely unaware of the psychological impact of the technology they are using to colonize.

INSTANTANEITY

Instantaneity, a function of globalization, imposes acceleration on all human societies. There are two principal effects of instantaneity: one is instant reach and feedback, the other is the elimination of an adaptation period. The first effect turns us into electronic nomads: it puts us in touch with any point in the world and retrieves information instantly from any point in the world. Ultimately our electric ubiquitousness will be positive and necessary, but currently it is causing a dangerous secondary effect; before we have the time to reorganize our own lives, to fashion our institutional response, the social, political and cultural consequences of technological innovations are upon us. We are not prepared to deal with these consequences.

Some regions of the world are trapped in a social time-warp, the legacy of neglect or coercion from dead or dying empires. We were caught unawares by the overnight disintegration of the Soviet Union, now we are helpless witnesses to local atrocities. We lack the psycho-political criteria and the emotional precision to cope with real, obscene human suffering. The loss of the necessary time delay in modern communications places all cultures in a condition of permanent jet-lag.

The problem is that, previously, in the days of print technology, social orders did fall into place, at the cost of huge human losses and after much pushing and shoving at geographical and institutional borders. Today, the new social order cannot be left to come of its own accord. The difference between today and yesterday is that while yesterday's boundaries were predicted on geography, hardware and solar time divisions, today, they depend entirely on psychological conditions. Thinking, feeling and expressing in culture and technology are what runs the world today, not military might.

CHANGING MODERN IDENTITY...

To this day we have not yet shaken the habit of centring ourselves as visual projections within the stage of our own imagination. Consequently we have no model for our own presence in the midst of fabricated, multiplied and transformed images of our selves in the electronic networks of the world.

Furthermore, ever since the invention of the photograph and its derivatives—from cinema to virtual reality—we have displaced, technologized and multiplied our point-of-view. With neural networks appearing on the technological horizon, much of our judgement faculties, once the exclusive preserve of personal and group deliberation, will increasingly be delegated to our technological extensions. True, the kind of technological subjectivities supported by neural networks will be crude at first, responding to simple criteria and selecting uncomplicated subjects. But this experimentation will lead very quickly to embryonic forms of autonomous consciousness. The commercial applications of endowing Personal Digital Agents (PDAs) with initiative and judgement will push the software industry to produce electronic mindservants.

Soon enough, the political problems attending the applications of complex neural networks in industry, medicine, business, banking, education and government services will bring about enough contradictions to require a fundamental psychological restructuring of our collective and personal minds. Where will that leave us? How will we know where, how and who we are when both our points-of-view and our judgements are computer-assisted and distributed over large databases in virtual time and space?

...FROM THE POINT-OF-VIEW...

While our sensory feedback extends well beyond our skin, we have not expanded our body-image accordingly. When I telephone from Toronto to Munich, I instantly become a 7,000-kilometre-wide blind man. When I use videoconferencing I am more completely "there," in the distant room that contains my video image, than when I am simply using the phone. Indeed, in the simulation and extensions of our nervous systems, replete with technological prostheses for vision, hearing, touch and, now even smell, we personally figure as nodal entities, travelling back and forth on electric current patterns that are co-extensive with our biological and neurological make-up. How do we account for this in psychological terms? What does it do to my self-image? It is obvious that, in order to be effective in this new context, we must project and reflect our self-images beyond representation. Or, at the very least, beyond visual representation.

A recent dialogue between Stelarc, an Australian artist, and Paul Virilio, a post-deconstructionist critic and media theorist, led Virilio to speculate on a new form of political and economic colonization, already theoretically possible, that would invade the body itself on a biological, genetic basis. Virilio's fear is justified, especially when one considers that big pharmaceutical companies are busy buying patents for pieces of our genetic puzzle. Furthermore, Stelarc's own ideological discourse on his work is not reassuring. He suggests, like

Hans Moravec and the cyberpunk generation, that the body is obsolete, and should be entirely replaced by technology. This is inverted romanticism, very far from the underlying psychology of our incipient technological symbiosis. Most electronic technologies are not leading to the abandonment of the body, but to the remapping of our sensory life to accommodate a combination of private and collective mind.

...TO THE POINT-OF-BEING

Our proprioceptive appreciation of reality involves the whole body and all the senses. Its point of reference is neither representation nor pure vision. The way I relate to the world of instant and pervasive communications is from my point-of-being, not my point-of-view. There is only one place where I am completely there, and that is within my own skin, even though that skin and its technologically assisted sensory extensions reach far beyond the immediate limits of vision, touch and hearing. My point-of-being is not exclusive but inclusive; it is not a perspective vision that frames reality, but rather, is a place defined by the precision and complexity of my connections with the world.

Only the last shreds of our erstwhile visual bias can still prevent us from recognizing the obvious: interactivity is touch. Industry is developing technological prostheses that act as multi-sensory integrators. Interactive technologies provide the social, psychological and physical bonds for the much larger collective intelligence. The collective mind that we are building now can handle the complexity, breaks and restructurings of individual minds—a world scale integration process is at work.

These new psychological criteria allow us to rethink the meaning of technological extensions, not as mere auxiliaries of signal transportation, but as forms, patterns and configurations of relationships. Potentially, all electronic technologies are interactive; they establish continuous intimate exchanges of energy and processing between our many bodies and minds and their global environment.

PUBLIC SPACE
AND PUBLIC SPHERE

Just when we thought we had pretty well got reality under control, it is changing again. It changed from the Middle Ages to the Age of Reason, and now, it is changing again to the Age of Mind. In the era of the book, the control of language was always private, but with electronic media the control of language became public and oral. Now, with the advent of the Internet we have the first medium that is oral and written, private and public, individual and collective at the same time. The connection between public and private mind is done via the open and connected networks of the planet. We will soon recognize that reality and this "public" mind are the same. We will have to tolerate and regulate the fact that the mind will gain more power over reason. However, just as religion was kept around during the era following the invention of print, so will reason be kept alive during the era of collective intelligence.

Politically, however, it is still unclear what system will correspond to this new order of collective intelligence and social behaviour. Business appears to be the collective mind that is presently in charge. It obeys laws that are consistent and universal. As well, business is a self-adjusting and self-balancing system of technology transfer. By and large, it seems to be good for us. However, the major flaw in business is its extremely poor environmental record and its reliance, in part, on military industries. Over 25 percent of the economy in almost all the advanced information states is founded on arms manufacturing and/or distribution. This is quite intolerable in a healthy mind, particularly the collective mind we are aspiring to become in the nearest possible future.

The good news is that, within the general orbit of advanced, industrial-military complex nations, business is gradually superseding the military influence over politics. Wherever the old order still prevails, long-suffering inhabitants are pining for the laws of business, which, on the surface at least, seem to be kinder than the others. A world where everybody is doing business with everybody else appears to be quite viable, if not always hugely inspired.

Technology drives business but also changes it. The Internet has startled the business world and puzzled governments. The 'Net is clearly on its way to becoming an electronic data superhighway, but it doesn't really want to be that. As an expression of a collective mind, the 'Net, of course, is much more sophisticated than anything we have ever known before.

In parallel with the expansion of the Internet, TV will undergo its own metamorphosis. After it consummates its marriage with the computer, TV will gradually privatize to the point of absurdity, losing its present grip on public space. Not too long from now, our sense of belonging to a common ground will come principally not from TV nor from physical space, but from our connection to the Internet or whatever the Internet presages.

The relationship between the individual and the collective is changing, and so are the rules governing their association. The old regime, based on open neutral space and space management in politics and the economy, must give way to a new regime based on address, speed and access controls. Speed of processing will cost more than space. A new consciousness of time is developing, as if, after having conquered space and made it less constraining, technological evolution was addressing time, real, virtual, personal and social, as the new frontier. From the evidence of daily developments in technology and overnight changes in the geopolitical economy of the Earth, we can conclude that we are still caught within the acceleration mode. And, although a kind of plateau is not too distant on the wavefront of culture, it is still hard to see it. In a true proprioceptive sense, what is happening is almost easier to feel than to see.

It is essential that as we develop networked communications we also create political mechanisms to protect universal access and freedom of expression as well as right to privacy on the 'Net. The recent attempt by the U.S. government to introduce a digital coding system (for which it carried a universal key) should be warning enough. It would be preferable, for example, if the U.S. decided, once and for all, to cease its logistical support of the Internet, and for other countries, for the sake of their own intellectual and political freedom, to get together and pick up the tab. It could be the first and the simplest way to ensure that democracy is continued in this new environment. In the near future any order that prevails on the 'Net will be that which prevails in reality, and whatever we can do now to prevent a global seizure must be considered.

COLLECTIVE INTELLIGENCE

The notion of collective intelligence came to me recently. Because it is a concept that is bound to grab at least some of the scientific community's attention, it is worth telling how I saw it develop. Early in November, 1994, I was at a party at *Mediamatic* magazine, in Amsterdam, to conclude a well-attended conference on design and the new technologies, "@Home." Though many speakers were truly illuminating, some of us were concerned that, perhaps, not enough attention had been paid to fundamental issues on the Internet: copyright, privacy, civil liberties, consumerism and commercialization, government interference, E-money, and other matters that are probably going to affect our lives in a fast approaching future. And though the emphasis was on design, some could argue that, for an increasing number of people, the Internet is becoming home, too.

At that party, I ran into a strategy analyst for AT&T named Phil Chang, whom I mistook for someone else. I started talking quite excitedly about Japan, implying that, naturally, I assumed he was Japanese. After a few minutes, he took advantage of a rare moment of silence to kindly inform me that he was in fact of Korean origin and that he had made San Francisco his home. To help me recover from my embarrassment, he asked me what had been so exciting in my encounter with the Japanese culture. I answered that, as soon as one walked down a street in Tokyo, one could feel the intelligence in the air. Seen from a foreigner's point of view, Tokyo seems to behave in sync, as if everybody knew and took in account what everybody else was doing. The level of coordination and tacit agreement experienced there reminded me of how I felt about the kind of people I had met at another venue, the 1994 International Symposium of Electronic Arts (ISEA) in Helsinki. Almost everybody there was "on the net." They felt like an altogether new kind of people. Moreover, it felt like a new kind of space. I realized then that the space of the 'Net was "alive" with an active, vibrant and human collective presence. Yes, there was something in common between ordinary people in the streets in Tokyo and the 400 artists-engineers gathered in Helsinki. Searching for the "mot juste," I said it was a kind of "collective intelligence."

At that precise moment, Jill Scott, an Australian multimedia artist, jumped up and cried "CI ! CI!, what a likely field of study." CI was created right then and there in the office of *Mediamatic*. Six of us gathered together and began to work: Jill; Phil; Josephine Greaves, another Australian artist who invited us to concentrate on the Net as the ideal playing field for CI; Erkki Huhtamo, one of the organizers of the Helsinki congress, who suggested we might consider "Chicken Intelligence" to stand behind CI, and David D'Heilly, who picked on the chicken idea as a "politically correct" mascot for the new science by letting out the most terrifyingly loud chicken yell I or anybody in the room had ever heard.

CI as a potentially scientific research concept was actually found by Jill Scott, but, for a while, I sincerely believed that *I* had come up with the idea of "collective intelligence," only to discover, a couple of weeks later, that the notion had already been entertained by Pierre Lévy, and that he had just published a book about it.[98] I am very happy about that, not only because it means that the idea is serious, but also because I don't have to write a book about it myself.

But now the notion has taken hold of me and it has opened up a whole new understanding of what it is that I have been searching for during all these years since I first asked questions about the alphabet.

Like all of us, I am both judge and party to the present condition of a mind whose history is continuous and has been growing like an organism for several millennia.

CHAPTER EIGHTEEN

CHANGING OUR MINDS

A BRIEF HISTORY OF INTELLIGENCE

LANGUAGE WAS OUR FIRST TECHNOLOGY

NFORMATION processing begins with spoken language. Language is still the most powerful code available to humans and will remain the principal one for the foreseeable future. As virtual reality developer Jaron Lanier explained to Frank Biocca: ". . . spoken language (. . .) is an extraordinary living construction. It is not just a technological project but a biological, evolutionary one. The (human) species has been sort of co-sprung with it. It's a part of our brains. It's physiologically part of us, and something that is profoundly deep and mysterious."99 What makes Lanier's observation better than the usual platitudes on the central role of language is that it underlines the profound intimacy that linguistic forms entertain with our biological make-up. Language is bred within us and helps us to form the thoughts that let us perceive reality and survive in it. The better we learn to control language, the better we are equipped to recognize, understand and live in the environments that constitute our reality. This is the stuff of human intelligence. Anything affecting the growth and development of language in us also affects the growth and development of intelligence.

WHY ALL LANGUAGE IS
PRETTY MUCH ARTIFICIAL

The evolution of human intelligence keeps pace with the evolution not only of language, but of technologies supporting and processing language. First among these is writing. While it is conceivable that the origin of language could be found in the practice of associating sounds with daily survival activities, it is writing that stored these sounds for enduring uses. By being written down, pertinent and selective oral practices achieved enough consistency and reliability for linguistic coding to develop over and beyond common usage. In evolutionary terms, one of the principal effects of writing language down, whatever system or code was being used, has been to detach human utterances from the speakers and allow them to be manipulated. In the previous, exclusively oral culture, language controlled people and their behaviour; with writing, the reverse became true. Societies that could read and write achieved a degree of control over language that allowed them to gain a new kind of mastery over their destinies.

WRITING AMPLIFIES
HUMAN COGNITION

Writing enabled humans to store, expand and exploit language as a medium of symbolic and practical control over reality. Writing, which is always at the core of specific strands of civilization, seems to act as kind of "intelligence amplifier," and it gives way to sudden bursts of cultural acceleration. As Harold Innis demonstrated in his impressive historical review of the impact of communications on culture, it is writing and the means of transporting messages that have provided for the conditions of social organization, codes of law and patterns of behavior.[100] But Eric Havelock's work has also shown that some languages, and especially some writing systems, such as the Greco-Roman alphabets, have tended to give individuals, rather than just society in general, more control than others. This matter directly affects the patterns of distribution of human intelligence that have prevailed in western societies.[101]

THE CODE IS THE MESSAGE

The kind of human intelligence developed in western civilization owes much of its shape to the specific coding methods of the western alphabets. Havelock's work indicates that the issue of alphabetic literacy was not just a matter of content, that is, a simple question of making more ideas or notions accessible to memory and mental rumination, but primarily an issue of processing. Havelock makes us perceive the alphabetic system, and all ancient writing systems, as we would perceive the merits of a computer code today, not only on the basis of what it could be used for, but on the basis of how it works in the processing platforms that support it. Like syllabaries, alphabets are phonological codes. This means that they don't represent images, concepts or ideas, but words themselves in their pronounceable linguistic forms. Hence, any writing that translates the actual sounds pronounced in spoken language into equivalent grapheme-to-phoneme representations makes the subtleties of grammar and vocabulary available for transcription, analysis and reworking. They give access to the articulations of language; they multiply the possibilities of variations on basic patterns of common usage.

As Havelock explains, alphabetic codes are much more powerful than syllabaries because, instead of analyzing spoken languages in terms of fully pronounceable syllables, they carry this analysis to the level of the individual phonemes. This has the effect of reducing the number of characters needed for the full representation of spoken words and also of eliminating ambiguities in complex syllabic contractions. The simpler, the more faithful the code, the more powerful a tool it is for taking fully conscious control over language. Havelock suggests that the refinements of the Greek alphabet upgraded the status of writing from that of a tool for memory to that of a tool for thinking. Human intelligence was released from the burden of remembering to be applied to innovating.[102]

THE REDISTRIBUTION OF HUMAN INTELLIGENCE IN PRIVATE SELVES

This was a monumental step for the development of rationality in the application of cognitive processing to the realm of nature, but it wasn't the most important impact of alphabetic writing on human intelligence. From their reliable spatio-temporal cognitive organization, the ancient Greeks also developed a very strong sense of themselves as observers of the reality they thus displayed in their minds. Simply by allowing for recording and archiving vital and factual information, any writing system could conceivably introduce and support various degrees of collective historical consciousness. Similarly, although they could not all be credited with supporting to the same degree the appreciation of depth perspective and 3-D spatialization, all visual writing systems emphasized spatial cognition at one level or another. What alphabetic literacy achieved to an unprecedented level was to feed back a very strong degree of self-consciousness to those who practised it.

To understand how that happened, we can refer either to the growing number of autobiographies by noted individualists such as Saint Augustine or Montaigne, or to the standard diaries kept by romantic or literate-minded schoolchildren. Anybody who writes a diary is both taking control of language and making use of it to develop a growing sense of selfhood. Writing down one's own thoughts, whether they concern oneself directly or are musings about reality or social observations, has the immediate consequence of defining one's relationship to reality and of reinforcing one's point of view on that reality. It is a faithful, constant and articulate mirror of one's own consciousness. It is an accelerator of one's intelligence. It is also an appropriation both of language in its structural detail and of information-processing. What the alphabet accomplished in the Greek, then Roman, then all western empires was to endow each and every reading citizen with a personal handle on reality and intelligence. Reading and writing are the fundamental conditions for the privatization of mind.

THE PAIN OF RESTRUCTURING

The privatization of mind initiated by literacy had disastrous consequences on established methods of collective information-processing run by religious and political hierarchies. Indeed, whereas other formal writings systems such as Egyptian hieroglyphs and Chinese ideograms put social information-processing under the control of political and religious hierarchies in top-down structures that left little room for individual input and initiative, one of the first effects of Greek literacy was to introduce a radically new political and social concept—democracy. Whether it was rigorously applied along the lines developed in Plato's Republic is not the point. What is critical is to understand how human intelligence, heretofore managed on a collective basis, suddenly became available for personal use and manipulation using the Greek alphabet. Political democracy begins first and foremost with psychological democracy.

Marshall McLuhan[103] and Elizabeth Eisenstein[104] both observed that the invention of the printing press (which greatly accelerated the impact of manuscript alphabetization) was at the root of the murderous religious upheavals during and after the Renaissance. The transition from the collective consciousness of the middle ages, predicated on the common goal of community salvation, to the new social order of public space and private minds took several centuries of fierce ideological and political strife.

In the end, human intelligence gained the conditions for unprecedented acceleration and growth. The concept of "nature," as developed by Greek philosophy, was a kind of space-time bubble for amplified and organized cognition. Nature became the realm of applied "common sense," but it has never been other than a cognitive consensus based on sharing in the heritage of alphabetic literacy. The scientific process cast aside religious dogma to constitute a clear separation between "objective" and "subjective" appreciation of reality. The objectification of common knowledge—stored in books, treatises, dictionaries, universities and libraries—guaranteed a common, public, social and mental space for the free evolution of individual contribution. Research initiatives and theories issuing from private citizens were put to the test of how cogent they were within the common lore. The standard test recognized by all was the causal, mechanical principle. If the theory or the experiment reflected and respected the normalized unfolding of consequences issuing from a hypothetical primal cause without disturbing established scientific paradigms, it was included in the encyclopaedia of human knowledge. If not, it was simply rejected without the theorist being beheaded. Heads were allowed to be wrong.

In this situation, the structural principles of social organization reflected and reinforced their sources in the community-based association of private minds.[105] Just as the common public space was structured on the understanding that material space was a neutral and infinite expanse within which the universe unfolded according to immutable mechanical laws, individual consciousness was organized in a spatial disposition commensurate with the space of everyday life. The other coordinate, time, was clearly distinguished from space, both in public historical records and in the philosophy of history, and in private psychological constructs. In personal reflections, the format of temporal sequencing was applied routinely to account for personal as well as historical life situations. Although the rapid acceleration of innovations in pure and applied science and technology always posed a threat to the established order, the cognitive situation remained relatively stable until the appearance of electricity.

MONEY MAKES THE WORLD
TICK LIKE A CLOCK

A subsidiary but not unimportant processing consequence of the invention of alphabetic literacy was the contemporary invention of minted money.[106] However, while ancient money was still very much tied to its roots in barter and direct exchange of usage values, the minted coins invented by the alphabetically literate Lydians during the seventh century BC reflected the structural principle of representation. This principle was installed as a cognitive subroutine by use of the alphabet. Just as the relationship between reading and meaning is predicated on the representation of abstract signifieds by equally abstract signifiers, the relationship between minted or printed money and value was centred not on the acquisition of real goods and services, but on the parsing and measuring of abstract value. This allowed money to become one of the main tools of human intelligence. New abstract valuation attitudes soon tipped the balance between usage and exchange values. In the history of western valuation processes, money became the universal translation system of most goods and services. The point to be made here is not to pick up where Marxist analysis left off, but to observe that money soon became human intelligence's way of parsing time, space and individual human effort. When Machiavelli suggested that "Every man has a price," he was not only prefiguring today's habit of measuring a person's "net worth," he was also alluding to the age-old practice of parsing human energy in terms of salaries. Money was human intelligence's parsing mechanism: it allowed it to keep track of and differentiate between portions of space, stretches of time and outputs of human energy. Money played in society the role of the timing clock in the central processing unit of the computer—synchronizing all the calculations of the computer.[107]

ELECTRICITY AND THE IMPLICATION OF TIME SPACE AND SELF

The telegraph was the first information-processing technology to reduce time and space constraints to instant communication. Consequently it had an almost immediate impact on co-ordinating and harmonizing human activities that, until its invention, had been conducted separately. It affected the pricing systems of goods and services and it affected the making and reporting of news. It also introduced new possibilities for the unfolding and the processing methods of human intelligence.

It is important to acknowledge the telegraph as the processing link between the alphabet and the computer. The translation of the twenty-six letters of the alphabet into three signs, long-short-nought, amounted to a radical refinement of the code, even as international wiring established the first model of a "common carrier" for networked intelligence. Of course, in order to achieve the universal flexibility of the binary code, a further reduction from three to two signs was critical. The continuity between the alphabet and the digit is reflected not only in the universal standards of the ASCII norms, but more pertinently in the fact that all computer operations until the appearance of neural network simulators have been based on the same fundamental principles of fragmentation, decontextualization and recombination.*

FRAGMENTATION

The discovery of phonemes, the smallest units of sound in language, was the inspiration that led early Greek philosophers to imagine the related notion of the atom. Fragmentation as the quest for the smallest distinguishing feature and/or the smallest common denominator of matter and information was a principle already applied by Plato for the analysis of human discourse, over two thousand years before Descartes gave it a formal dressing in his foundational *Method*. The same principle was applied more recently to arrive at the smallest

---

* Neural networks, especially those that are based on analogue chips, are quite different in that they operate on the basis of context and contextualizing data, while all other computer architectures adopt the principle of fragmentation as the basis of their operations.

distinguishing features of the physiological and chemical components of life forms. Phonemes, atoms and genes partake of the same conceptual processing strategy. Of course, it is demonstrably possible and perhaps necessary to fragment them even further, but there is no percentage in cutting up the binary digit. Today, digitization has superseded both money and the alphabet as the main parsing device. It is the new universal translator of all heterogeneous substances. However, in and of itself, fragmentation was not enough to liberate matter and information for analysis and re-use. The principle had to be supported by its corollary, decontextualization.

DECONTEXTUALIZATION AND RECOMBINATION

The Greek alphabet was different from practically every other writing system in the world. Instead of obliging the reader to stick to the meaningful context of the displayed text, it allowed one to remove statements from their points of origin and to place them elsewhere, in other, not previously related contexts. Interestingly enough, this characteristic is supported by the cognitive processes involved in reading itself. You can easily decipher and even read aloud any alphabetical string without having a clue of what it is actually saying, but you cannot do that with Hebrew, Arabic, hieroglyphs or ideograms. The principle of decontextualization is also supported by the neurophysiological response to deciphering criteria. The contiguous sequences of alphabetic letters are self-supporting and hence are strung laterally in the right visual fields of both eyes, while the need to search for contextual cues forbids readers of other writing systems to separate the meaning from the code. With alphabetic orthography, the text is freed from its context. Obviously, this principle of decontextualization is also present, of necessity, in all machine language codes. Together, fragmentation and decontextualization form the basis for recombination, which is the source of the typically western drive for innovation, the well that, in *Finnegans Wake*, James Joyce called the "Cartesian spring."

I have purposely borrowed the term "recombinant" from genetic engineering because it helps us to recognize that the alphabet and related codes behave like the RNA—otherwise known as the "messenger genes"—of living cells. By analyzing (fragmenting) matter and language, excerpting (decontextualizing) useful segments, and then combining (recombining) them with other segments, western cultures have tended to practise innovation as a survival strategy. This has led to quantum leaps in the applications of human intelligence to social, cultural and technological situations.

SELF

Because we carry within ourselves the self-image inherited from the literate-based Renaissance, we fail to recognize that all electronic technologies, from the telephone to VR, extend our physical being well beyond the limits of our skin. The question of proprioception, our sense of our bodily outline, will soon emerge as the key psychological issue confronting the new generation of technologically aware people. Indeed, just as the rapid elaboration of the point-of-view became the condition for individual freedom in the neutral space of Renaissant perspectivism, a proprioceptive appreciation for one's point-of-being in networked data flow is among the conditions for retaining a measure of physiological and psychological control over one's whereabouts in electronic nomadism. In that regard, novelist William Gibson's notion of people "jacking into cyberspace" is truly prophetic.*

On the other hand, the traditional boundaries between what is inside and what is outside in all computerized interactions is quite problematic and perhaps will become increasingly irrelevant as the

---

* There are many instructive references to unprecedented tactile experiences in Gibson's *Neuromancer* (New York: Ace Book, 1984); especially relevant to an understanding of what we are getting into is the suggestion that one could conceivably "ride" another person's or a robot's "body" in radical telepresence.

big Renaissance picture flips into its opposite. As Lanier explained to Biocca,

> I think one of the striking things about a virtual world system in which you have the pliancy, the ability to change the content of the world easily, is that the distinction between your own body and the rest of the world is slippery. Essentially, from a virtual reality perspective, the definition of the body is that part which you can move as fast as you think. In a virtual world (. . .), you might be opening doors at a distance or exploding volcanoes on the horizon, or whatever it might be. At that point, it becomes difficult to really define what the boundary of the body is.[108]

Lanier's observation could apply just as well to the telephone or to videoconferencing, although these media do not make it quite so obvious.

Among the most pertinent observations of artists about new images of selfhood arising from cyberactive systems is David Rokeby's notion of "borrowed subjectivity." Not only is it possible to record and play back someone else's sensory experience in a VR environment, but, as Jaron Lanier has often observed, the feedback effect of modulated outputs from one's activity in VR can distort one's sense of self as surely as a drug or a spin in a cyclotron. The difference, of course, is that the VR experience is both controlled and fully analyzable. Changing selves may well become the most valued form of entertainment of tomorrow.

THE NEW "COMMON CARRIER"

The idea of borrowed subjectivity in VR is only an extreme example of what is already common in networked communications. Their effect is to expand the self from its private mental space into on-line shared mental space, while retaining the immediate social space for privacy. Logging in and out of the Internet amounts to spreading oneself in cyberspace and out of time, especially in asynchronous transfer modes. The "on-line self" is supported by neither time, space nor body, and yet is unmistakably present.* Furthermore, word-processing, whether in stand-alone workstations or on-line, is really "thought-processing," just as wordsmithing in the old literate mode was a kind of slowed-down, itemized and personalized but on-going and shareable cognitive development. The acceleration of feedback, the concentration of many individual inputs in computer conferences, the instant redistribution of data for group rumination generates new patterns of mediation and intermediation. The boundaries between subjective input and objective assimilation open up to new interjective communities of mind.

The space-time-self bubble of the literate cognition, separating clearly the objective and subjective realities of cognitive agents, is now being reversed. Electronic highways and superhighways are merging into a single common cognitive environment where the individual user, at once a consumer and a producer, becomes a kind of ubiquitous, floating neural/nodal entity. In that new configuration, the world outside is neither fixed nor "real" in the conventional sense, but behaves like an active super- or hyper-consciousness in permanent flux and change and adjustment to local needs and circumstances. For this evolving arch-cognitive environment, in spite of the unending struggle of the industry to maintain control by multiplying proprietary standards, the ultimate and inexorable trend will be to provide a universal global common carrier based on the image of the telephone network. Digitization provides the universal common substance, the "common sense" of the common carrier.

---

* Internet users often delight in the absence of physiological features to interfere with the assumed "authenticity" of their communications. Many of the electronic pornographers who run on-line sexual conversations, for profit, in France's notorious "Minitel rose" advertise themselves on large public billboards as pretty young blondes but are, in fact, little old men in back offices.

CHAPTER NINETEEN

PSYCHOTECHNOLOGIES

"Electric speed tends to abolish time and space in human awareness. There is no delay in the effect of one event upon another. The electric extension of the nervous system creates the unified field of organically interrelated structures that we call the present Age of Information."

— Marshall McLuhan

E LECTRONIC MEDIA are immediate, unifying fields. Marketing analysts and electronic pollsters orchestrate our collective, electronic emotions. Via TV and radio, a planetary event like the Gulf crisis grabs the attention of the whole world, usually to the exclusion of any local concerns. During the war itself, our opinions were controlled by decisions on the media front as much as any on the military front, though live TV by-passed military censors on several occasions. This was collective, techno-cultural morality in action. Under the gaze of satellites, large trade blocs are forming within continental boundaries. These expand our identity beyond personal, local, national and even linguistic boundaries. Globalizing the economy may well be necessary—a continuous metaphor even—for the globalization of our personal psychology through the extension of psychotechnologies. The most interesting question here is: how does the individual relate to such a situation?

WITH TV, IMAGINATION
HAPPENS OUTSIDE YOUR MIND

With TV, the point of view is without, looking right into you with a beam of electrons. TV is a very public point of view. It invites people to make sense outside their own mind: that is, to receive fully constituted images of the social discourse from the outside in. When the western world was ruled by books alone, there was an "inside" and an "outside" to our psychological experience. The outside realm was public, collective, stable, reliable and objective. It was institutionalized by law, education and science. The inside realm of our minds remained private, personal and subjective.

The live media, however, such as radio and TV, have accelerated external information-processing and begun to blur the distinction between private and public. If reading print is a truly private experience, listening to radio, watching television or logging onto the Internet is not.

TV supplies a kind of "mental" reality outside the body and the mind. While you watch TV, if your mind doesn't wander, if you don't hold a remote control, the screen images replace your own. You share in the collective imagination and the collective thinking it makes available to you. On television, the images do not come from personal experience, but from the work of a professional production team, often strongly influenced by polls and market surveys. Polls deal not with particulars or individual tastes and choices, but with numbers. Thus polling and the television fare that depends upon it is addressed to the collective rather than the private consciousness.

NEITHER HERE NOR THERE

When watching TV, of course, we have to abstract from the images a certain, albeit minimal, sense. Even though there isn't much room for other mental activity. Our job is to interpret the sequence of images and sounds in much the same way as we do in life: by making sense of what is happening second by second. The televised psychological reality cannot really be described as objective. By bringing the outside world inside the home, television provides an intermediate level of social discourse, neither exclusively public, nor really private; neither frankly fictional, nor reliably real. We may not yet be fully aware of this. In spite of the pressure to adopt external psychological models, we were still brought up on books, hence we are still able to sustain the models of private consciousness developed during the Renaissance.

TELEVISION— OUR COMMON ELECTRONIC SENSE

It doesn't matter whether we have one channel or fifty. The content of one TV station will usually echo another. Apart from matters of style, television discourse is the same the world over. TV is a barometer of global, if not local, psychology. It is our global electronic psychology providing us with common notions of time, space and society. Television provides all of us with a psychotechnological moral envelope. By selecting the topics of our moral consciousness, it also does some of our thinking for us. Armies of reporters and advertisers help to sort out what's worth saying and what isn't. We are interwoven into a mass psychology that selects our issues for us and unifies us in convergent opinions. TV doesn't take chances with public morality. When a controversial issue comes up, such as whether to question or even defy a government decision, North American and European TV stations appear to be endowed with a sort of automatic system of standardization and self-censorship. The news on one channel is often identical, item for item, to what's being reported on another. During the Gulf War, TV, acting as a trend setter and arbiter of public morality, had the effect of increasing the number of people in favour of the war in the U.S., Canada and Europe (initially 55 percent, later 85 percent).

Collectively and daily, we look for continuity, security and equilibrium. Public morality is worked out live on TV. Selected issues are supported by simple narratives everyone can relate to. We begin to get a sense of the collective mind, not as a concept, but as an active process responding immediately to events as they happen. Neither real nor fabricated, neither public nor private—but all these things at once—all information is summed up in the television moment.

The sum total of all the talk on our screens is our new, electronic common sense. Truly common in that it is made up by public media. Truly sensory in that it is a reflexive sense organ. TV, and to some extent radio, operate as the ruminations of nations. Indeed, the average news report—a short 20–45 second clip—corresponds exactly to the time most people can afford to devote to such issues.

When all the commentaries from all the newscasts about a certain issue are considered as a whole, they can be truly perceived as "the Nation thinking" and this common sense is fed into the pattern and organization of culture. TV is also the privileged medium for working out our relationships to collective reality. There used to be a time when you were told never to believe anything you had seen in print. Now you see it first on TV. According to statistics, television is considered today to be the most important, the most believable, the most "authoritative" medium. It is well worth considering that common sense is the tacit agreement between individuals and society in a stable democratic environment.

McLuhan was the first to recognize "that electric information systems are live environments in the full organic sense. They alter our feelings and sensibilities, especially when they are not attended to."[109] What happens when our common sense is no more within ourselves, but without?

THE INTEGRATION OF
TV AND COMPUTERS

Television is not alone any more. Our passive relationship to an "objective" screen is over; computers have introduced a whole new series of relationships—interfaces—between people and screens.

Our machines talk to us and expect answers. Furthermore, because computers intensify and tighten the relationships between all the electronic media, integrated media are changing and expanding the ground of human psychology.

Computers mediate between the internal nervous system of individual users and external processing systems: they act as interfaces between the psychological and the technical, just as video games provide interfaces between the neurological and the electronic responses. This interaction is an example of a close biotechnical exchange. Electricity, which is produced both organically and technologically, is the common ground. Electricity is also the medium that hooks up the whole world into a single network. The local biotechnical exchanges between body, mind and machine are now linked to the global environment by data processing and worldwide relays. The real object of computerization is to extend to the electronic environment the kind of control and monitoring relationships people experience within themselves.

The new electronic media are becoming intermediate environments, accessing the intimate reality of our private psyches and providing a bridge to the outside world. They effect a kind of social mediation in a single continuous extension of our personal powers of imagination, concentration and action. They function largely like a second mind—one soon to be endowed with more autonomy than we might care for.

PSYCHOTECHNOLOGIES

We still tend to think of news and news reporting simply as items of processed information. The media that carry the news are perceived as neutral supports for storage and delivery, not as information processors. This view stems from our literate mindset, which takes print as the model information medium. With print, information is already complete. It is the reader who is the processor, the free agent. But now that machines are processing words and information for us, we may have to take a harder look at the relationship between our media and the perception of ourselves as autonomous consumers and producers of information.

Information-processing systems, such as computers and videos, are extensions of some of the main psychological properties of our minds. In this way, they can be called technologies of the psyche—psychotechnologies. Psychotechnologies include 'live' information-processing devices and networks, public and domestic. The telephone, radio, television, computers and satellites, for example. Since they change relationships within the fabric of society, they also restructure or modify psychological features, especially those that are dependent on interaction between language and the human organism or between mind and machine.

At the simplest level, any medium obliges us to respond physically to its way of working. For example, we have to sit down in front of a screen to watch television. But we also have to respond psychologically: we use our memory and imagination differently depending upon whether we are reading or listening to radio. At a deeper level, we have seen that our exposure to dominant media, such as books and television, may actually have secondary effects well beyond the time of the exposure itself, conditioning us both socially and psychologically to respond according to technical rather than exclusively psychological criteria.

TELECRACY

The power of the new media can already be demonstrated by the polls. While TV scans our mind, computerized polls scan the social body, leaving it like a skeleton on an X-ray negative. Aided by computers, television programming is related more closely to us by instant retrieval networks and monitoring systems. Indeed, polls, chart ratings, market surveys and all the other people meters generate a collective, average and averaging psychology, further homogenized by competition between broadcasters. With polls to work out TV's relationship with the collective, the integrated media become a kind of half-way consciousness, a comprehensive mediation between the self and the world, between them and us, between our brains and the stuff of life.

The integration of television and other news media within computer networks enables polling engineers to reduce the time interval between question and answer, between action and reaction. The potential for manipulating opinions, in such conditions, is greatly amplified. This has many political and social repercussions.

Increasingly, the politicians of western-style democracies owe their power base to meticulous computerized analyses of public opinion in any given arena. Campaign managers tailor their responses in locally appropriate media. During political campaigns the world over, TV stuffs its images into the electors' consciousnesses while computers analyze the polled responses, which are instantly presented as statistical facts. All this is supposed to help you make up your mind. But when television and computers are integrated in a single feedback loop on urgent issues, that mind is made up for you. Your own mind may hardly be involved at all.

It is one thing for polls to reflect, as accurately as possible, the opinions of a given community. It is quite another for the same polls to shape opinions, or present opinions which weren't there before. This is psychotechnology in action. Polls and statistics have a homogenizing effect on public opinion because they highlight, and thus promote, majority responses over dissent. In a culture where the means of making up one's mind are given less weight and time than those which make up the collective mind, it is easier to let the majority hold sway. This is one of the trade-offs between book and television culture.

SPIN-DOCTORING

French sociologist, Jean Baudrillard, suggests that, in the new media context, it is no longer necessary to *produce* opinion (as was the case in the Age of Enlightenment) but merely to *reproduce* public opinion.[110] To create a current of opinion, it is enough to raise an issue, say immigration or abortion, in the press and on TV. The next thing is to conduct an opinion survey. Often, the results of the initial poll are inconclusive. At that point, the media heat up the debate by exposing and highlighting any controversial story that will catch the public's attention. Such events, in themselves, are often trivial and statistically insignificant. When the time is ripe, usually after some triggering incident given prominence by TV or the press, another poll is taken and exposed. In no time at all, people feel that they have become authorities on an issue about which they had not the faintest idea a month before, and for which no new information has been forthcoming. In truth, many people decide on a hunch, not on facts. Many people, often those who constitute the "don't knows" are deeply influenced by what other people, especially people of influence, think and say. The undecided voters—usually between 15 and 20 percent of the electorate—are usually critical to a result. Therefore they are the prime target of election campaigns. To rope them in, the trick is to give the right weight, at the right time, in the right media, to the opinions of people of power and influence.

The last American elections introduced a new figure on the media scene, that of the "spin-doctor." The spin doctor is an opinion engineer, whose job is to "put a spin" on a leader's political views at press conferences and public meetings. The job consists of selecting and highlighting the words, sound-bites and sentences that are most likely to generate the desired effect on public opinion. Quoting and repeating, with or even without an appropriate commentary, is like starting a snowball. The spinning does the rest. Spin-doctoring would not work without electronic media. Electricity itself is a "spin." The reverberation or feedback from one medium to the next, from press to TV and back, creates an impression that quickly turns into an emotion and feeds an opinion. Another poll firms up the progress of the opinion, which in turn generates more support for the opinion. There is a general acceleration effect between the polling and reporting, especially when the second or third poll comes around.

As McLuhan quipped, "When information moves at electric speed, the worlds of trends and rumours become the 'real' world."[III] The point is that the new electronic elections are not a true representation of individual votes, more a case of the electronic environment amplifying and making real local opinions fed by spin-doctors. The environment is very sensitive to fluctuations, showing patterns of stimulation and reversal just like human emotions. It is the speed of response that turns the integrated electronic environment into a collective emotional system. Students of crowd psychology, media experts, advertising executives and polling engineers all agree: there is a considerable band-wagon effect that pushes the "don't knows" along the way of the assumed majority, particularly when the assumption is played out in the media. And, of course, politicians know perfectly well that undecided voters need to know about other voters' opinions before committing themselves.

SATELLITES AND THE NEW CONTINENTAL SENSIBILITY

It is also this indefinable quality of collective psychotechnological emotion that is changing our geopolitical and economic ground. Our geographical sensibility was once conditioned by models of stable national and continental boundaries in far away places. The geography of the Earth was a stage for relatively slow moving historical developments. Today this impression has to yield to images of fast changing climatic and political conditions affecting every local business in a real, monetary way. Satellites, not national boundaries, rule geographical configurations.*

---

* According to political economist David Linowes, there are over 3,000 communications satellites in space and, as A.C. Clarke once observed, a combination of any three of them can potentially reach every person on the planet.

The continental psychology—evidenced by ideas such as Europe 1992 or the 1993 Free Trade Agreement between Canada the U.S. and Mexico—may be one of the most important side effects of satellite technology.* Satellites have changed the viewpoint on local and global events. They are "God's eye," a panopticon made available to each and every one of us. Satellites ignore national boundaries and replace our customary land-based psychology with one that is predicated on large techno-cultural fields. The only boundaries they respect are those that separate populated and non-populated areas, such as land and sea, weighting continental perspectives. Satellites introduce a new sensibility and a new awareness of how we, the people, fit within the national and international consciousness. Satellites provide the world with a kind of electronic skin, sending and receiving sensitive information about human affairs in a large comprehensive network of relationships, bringing unity and transparency to our perceptions of ever increasing parts of the world.

On the other hand there is much room for diversity in the unified ensembles of the media synergy. Regarding the role of changing technologies in European broadcasting, German broadcast executive Hans Kimmel explains that

> new frequency bands, satellites and cable distribution have put an end to channel restrictions. Broadcasting monopolies are no longer possible and no longer required. Indeed the development of European broadcasting has been subjected to steady decentralization in spite of the protection afforded to national language stations.... the public is no longer faced with a solitary powerful God of Communications transmitting his monotheistic message via the television screen to pilgrims assembled nolens volens in his temple. No broadcaster is any longer in a

---

* The launching of the first series of completely European communication satellites, ECS-1, 2 and 3, sent into orbit by French Ariane rockets, between June 1983 and May 1985, provoked a flurry of regulatory activities to control usage and sharing of the airwaves by the member states.

position to address 'the Nation'. The remote-control has put an end to channel loyalty.[112]

The awareness of Europe as an entity has been accompanied and reinforced by a growing awareness of the role of the media as the new social bond. Now it's replacing less relevant national and ideological polarities.

PSYCHOTECHNOLOGICAL IDENTITIES

To go by the acronyms used for their European programs, like ESPRIT, BRITE, FAST, ERASMUS, MEDIA, BRAIN, SPRINT and EUREKA, you can see a tendency among bureaucrats to present their projects as a kind of "cognitive revolution." Indeed, the collective mind is finding expression, and the means to develop its own activities, in a techno-cultural field of human psychology and institutional telecommunications and audiovisual technology. This inclusive European mind is now in the making and we have exceptional opportunity to see its self-organizing processes in action. It is given substance by the *Single European Act*. It supports nine different languages and a thousand dialects. It is not a result of industrial or economic policy, but of the new technically assisted psychology of post-industrial culture. The networks of psychotechnological activities are provided by telecommunications. Their content, the myriad facets of European characteristics, is fed through the broadcasting media. Although the development of such large techno-cultural "minds" will soon be recognized as the mark of continentalism everywhere, we have yet to acknowledge this kind of psychological organization in North America.

On the other hand, if electronic communications have all but eliminated the significance of geographical boundaries as market interfaces, they are also eroding the boundaries between local and global identities. Electricity flows through peoples and cultures and rearranges them as it reconfigures techno-cultural fields. Just as electronic media bypass physical and geographical boundaries, the electronic flow also bypasses our personal boundaries. The scanner beam rubs out most of our psychological defences and erodes the walls of our private identity.

Because the structures of information delivery systems shape our psychological responses in formal ways (the medium here being the message), psychotechnologies create the condition for an expanded self, springing from the personal self to the farthest reaches of all that we can survey with our ever-expanding, all-probing perceptual and motor extensions.

I AM THE EARTH LOOKING AT ITSELF

Peter Russell began his book, *The Brain Book*, with a quote from the astronomer Fred Hoyle, "Once a photograph of the Earth, taken from outside, is available . . . a new idea as powerful as any in history will be let loose."[113] This quote is both true and appropriate for a book that breaks new ground in planetary perception. What is implied, of course, is that, upon seeing the photograph, we may get a feeling for the unity of the Earth and that of mankind upon it. We begin to realize that the Earth is a unified mass suspended in sidereal space. That photograph would initiate a new psychological state.

I remember that, as a child, having been exposed to dozens of representations of our planet in comics and schoolbooks, I was vaguely conscious of the fact that the Earth was a big round ball of matter suspended in space. These images were interesting but not really moving. And yet when I saw, much later, the first photograph of the Earth from space in *Paris-Match*, I experienced a fantastic emotion, a feeling of wonder and tenderness, and also a sense of radical contradiction: it was impossible that I was seeing this and yet I was indeed seeing it. The photograph was "the real thing," at least it was the most real access I could expect to the real thing. In the same way, photographs of the other side of the moon, or computerized reconstructions of the surface of Miranda give me the emotion of the real thing, of my own extension into space.

Surely, the most important effect of the photograph of the Earth is that it expands our perception of our self beyond our own body-image and enlarges our sense of identity. Indeed, from the first moment we see that photograph, we take possession of the Earth and of a new power to invest in it. It is an extension of my eyes. All that which is contained in it is 'of me' as much as I am 'of it.' It's me. With this photograph, I am given reliable evidence that I am all at once terribly big and terribly small. A paradox supported by the fact that I 'see' the Earth is that, though I am only one of five billion people, that enormous thing is part of me. The fact that I did not take that photograph myself, even the fact that it was taken by remote-control makes little difference. If something coming from this 'larger me' was sent there to make this photograph, then I also made it, along with all the people for whom it has a meaning.

In the same way, thanks to photography and television, going to the moon is now within my powers, even though I will never go there with my personal share of organic substance that I call my body. This feeling could not occur without a reliable technical extension of my very own perceptions. I could read about going to the moon in the papers, but it would be someone else's experience. Television makes it mine. The same argument goes for the telephone and other communication media that give me instant access to any point on the photograph; these extensions of my own senses search the body of the planet and make it part of me.

Thanks to this photograph, I am the Earth and so is everybody else. This is a new psychological experience with immense implications. The best revenge against psychotechnologies that would turn us into extensions of themselves is to include them within our personal psychology. A new human is in the making.

NOTES

1 June, 1989.

2 As Early C. Joseph explains, "Growth usually takes longer than is forecast. Despite the often touted belief that the world is changing ever faster, a review of past innovation shows that it still takes a long time for an innovation to find commercial success. For example, transistors were invented more than 40 years ago at Bell Labs. It took nearly a decade before the devices were used in computers and decades more before they made their way into consumer goods. The microwave oven, for example, took over 20 years to succeed. Long time-frames may also apply to the time a product takes to fade from the market. A study of the top 25 brands of the 1920s show that 23 of them are still number one in their product category." "Lessons from Past Errors," *Futures* (November 1990): 988–89.

3 NBC aired Bill Moyers' four-part series on "Television, the Public Mind" during the 1989 season.

4 Hertha Sturm, "Perception and Television: The Missing Half Second," *The Work of Hertha Sturm,* edited and translated from German by Gertrude J. Robinson (Montreal: McGill University, Working Papers in Communications, 1988), 39.

5 Edward R. Slopek, "Collapsing the Interval," *Impulse* (n.d.): 29–34.

6 Morris Wolfe, *Jolts: The TV Wasteland and the Canadian Oasis* (Toronto: James Lorimer and Co., 1985).

7 Eugene T. Gendlin, *Experience and the Creation of Meaning* (New York: Free Press, 1964), 27.

8 Jean-Marie Pradier, "Toward a Biological Theory of the Body in Performance," *New Theatre Quarterly* (February 1990): 89.

9 Tony Schwartz, *Media: The Second God* (Garden City, NY: Anchor Books, 1983).

10 Herbert E. Krugman, "Memory without Recall, Exposure without

Perception," *Journal of Advertising Research* 7:4 (August 1977): 8.

11 William S. Kowinski, *The Malling of America* (New York: William Morrow, 1985), 43–8.

12 Denise Schmandt-Besserat, "L'invention de l'écriture," *Les imaginaires, II, Cause commune* (1979): 119–30.

13 See D. de Kerckhove and C.J. Lumsden (eds.), *The Alphabet and the Brain, the Lateralization of Writing* (Heidelberg: Springer-Verlag, 1988); "A Theory of Greek Tragedy," *Sub-Stance* 29 (May 1981): 23–36; "Ecriture, théâtre et neurologie," *Etudes françaises* (Avril 1982): 109–28. D. de Kerckhove and D. Jutras (eds.), "Introduction à la recherche neuroculturelle," *McLuhan e la metamorfosi dell'uomo* (Ottawa: Canadian Commission for UNESCO, Occasional Paper 49, 1984), 112–29.

14 Joseph E. Bogen, "Some Educational Aspects of Hemispheric Specialization," *UCLA Educator* 17: 2 (1975): 29.

15 See Kerckhove and Lumsden, *Alphabet and the Brain*, especially "Logical principles underlying the layout of Greek Orthography," 153–72 and "Critical brain processes involved in deciphering the Greek alphabet," 401–21.

16 Talking to Jonathan Miller, Ernst Gombrich suggested that the refinement of perspectivist representation arose from a demand for realism that he calls the "eye-witness principle," the desire to represent and to see an event as if it were happening right there: "It was this demand which, twice in history (in the ancient world and in the Renaissance) led to . . . the imitation of nature through 'schema and correction,' through 'making and matching' by means of a systematic series of trial and error which allowed us finally to look across the flat picture surface into an imaginary world evoked by the artist." In J. Miller, *States of Mind* (New York, Methuen, 1983), 231.

17 Paul Levinson, "Media relations: Integrating computer telecommunications with education media," in R. Mason and T. Kaye (eds.) *Mindweave: Communication, Computers and Distance Education* (London: Pergamon, 1989), 42.

18 Laura Carrabine, "Plugging into the Computer to Sense Virtual Reality," *Computer-Aided Engineering* (June 1990): 23.

19 Marshall McLuhan, *Understanding Media* (Toronto: McGraw-Hill, 1964).

20 Howard Rheingold, "Travels in Virtual Reality," *Whole Earth Review* (Summer, 1990): 85.

21 Steve Pruitt and Tom Barrett, "The Corporate Virtual Workspace," paper presented at the First Conference on Cyberspace, May 4-5, 1991, Univer-

sity of Texas, Austin (from an unpublished report by Maurice Sharp, Knowledge Science Labs, University of Calgary).

22 Esther Dyson, *Forbes Magazine* (Sept. 17, 1990): 204.

23 John Perry Barlow, "Being in Nothingness," *Micro Times* (Jan. 22, 1990): 104.

24 Dyson, *Forbes Magazine*.

25 Pruit and Barrett, "The Corporate Virtual Workspace."

26 Quoted by Rheingold, "Travels in Virtual Reality."

27 Marc de Groot, "Virtual Reality," *Unix Review* 8:8 (August, 1990): 34–5.

28 Rheingold, "Travels in Virtual Reality," 82.

29 It is worth noting that it is a woman, not a man, who is presently considered the pioneer of electronic tactility. Margaret Minsky, daughter of a well-known MIT computer expert, is developing a leading-edge "virtual texture simulator" that, along with other systems for movement, weight and density simulation, will eventually increase the range and the depth of our tactile appreciation of objects both in and out of VR. As Steve Ditlea describes it, "Electrically stimulated crystals may be used at each fingertip to create a tingling sensation, which the human brain will interpret as pressure from a solid object," ibid., 94.

30 Jaron Lanier and Frank Biocca, "An Insider's View of the Future of Virtual Reality," *Journal of Communication* 42:4 (Autumn 1992): 160.

31 McLuhan, *Understanding Media*, 67.

32 Laura Carrabine, "Plugging into the Computer to Sense Virtual Reality," *Computer-Aided Engineering* (June 1990): 23, 26.

33 Barlow, "Being in Nothingness," 104.

34 Quoted by Eric Gullichsen, "In the Realm of the Sensors," *Catalogue of Art Futurea 1990* (Barcelona: Summer, 1990), 83.

35 It is not impossible to cause a short circuit in the process [of electro-chemical impulses] by substituting the stimulus of outer reality by a connection between the cerebral network and a computer program which sends stimuli similar to sensory preceptions. "Virtual Realities," ibid., 21.

36 Tom Perkings, as quoted by Scott Fisher, "Virtual Environments, Personal Simulations and Telepresence," ibid., 50.

37 Ibid., 51.

38 Ibid.

39 Nicholas Negroponte, "Trading places: Over the next 20 years, television and telecommunications will swap their primary means of transmission"

in "Products and Services for Computer Networks," *Scientific American* (September 1991): 76–8.

40 George Gilder, "The End of Telephony," *150 Economist Years*, special anniversary issue of *The Economist*, 1993.

41 Personal communication.

42 Mark Poster, *The Mode of Information* (Chicago: University of Chicago Press, 1990).

43 William Irwin Thompson, "History as Cultural Perception," *Understanding 1984/Pour comprendre 1984*, (Ottawa: Canadian Commission for UNESCO, Occasional Paper 48, 1984): 319.

44 Tom Forester, *High-Tech Society* (Cambridge, Mass.: MIT Press, 1988), 218.

45 As David F. Linowes comments: "Most Americans have no idea of the scope of personal, sensitive information about all of us now being accumulated and maintained in massive computer memories, never to be destroyed. They are held by business corporations, banks, insurance companies, government agencies, even schools and religious organizations." "The Information Age: Technology and Computers," *Vital Speeches Of the Day* (October 27, 1990).

46 Thompson, "History as Cultural Perception."

47 Philippe Quéau at a conference, "Babel," Cologne (November, 1992).

48 See Howard Rheingold, *Virtual Reality* (New York: Summit Books, 1991), 55–7.

49 Alvin Toffler, *The Third Wave* (New York: Morrow, 1980).

50 Jacques Attali, *Noise: The Political Economy of Music* (Paris: Le Seuil, 1989), 3.

51 Sandra Trehub and Bruce Schneider (eds.), *Auditory Development in Infancy* (New York: Plenum Press, 1985).

52 Alfred Tomatis, *L'oreille* (Paris: Le Seuil, 1972).

53 Jean-Pierre Chargeux, *Neuronal Man* (Boston: Basic Books, 1990).

54 Jacques Méhler, *Théories du langage, Théories de l'apprentissage* (Paris: Le Seuil, 1979).

55 Julian Jaynes, *The Origins of Consciousness in the Break-Down of the Bi-Cameral Mind* (Boston: Houghton Mifflin, 1976).

56 Marshall McLuhan, *The Gutenberg Galaxy* (Toronto: University of Toronto Press, 1962).

57 Walter Ong, *Orality and Literacy* (London: Methuen, 1982).

58 Marcel Mauss, *A General Theory of Magic* (London: Routledge and Kegan Paul, 1972).

59 Eric A. Havelock, *Preface to Plato* (Cambridge, Mass.: Belknap Press of Harvard University Press, 1963); *Prologue to Greek Literacy: Lectures in Memory of Louise* (Cincinnati: University of Cincinatti, 1971).

60 Diane McGuinness, "Sex, Symbols, and Sensation," in D. de Kerckhove and A. Iannucci (eds.) *McLuhan e la Metamorfosi Dell'uomo* (Ottawa: Canadian Commission for UNESCO, Occasional Paper No 49, 1984).

61 Sylvia Scribner and Michael Cole, *The Psychology of Literacy* (Cambridge, Mass.: Harvard University Press, 1981).

62 Personal communication.

63 The *Futurist*, (Sept.-Oct. 1989): 10.

64 According to Robert B. Porter, "In 1989, a ten-minute telephone call from the United States to the United Kingdom cost $9.90. In 1950, the same phone call cost $209.30, measured in 1989 dollars. It is no coincidence that the number of calls from the US to the UK rose from 110,300 in 1950 to almost 85 million in 1989." In "Conflict and Co-operation in the Global Marketplace," *Vital Speeches of the Day* 57: 6 (Jan. 1, 1991): 163.

65 Herb Brody, "The Neural Computer," *Technology Review* (Aug./Sept. 1990): 46.

66 Ibid.

67 J. Clarke Smith, "A neural network—could it work for you?" *Financial Executive* (May/June 1990): 26.

68 Maureen Caudill, "Humanly Inspired," *Unix Review* 7:5 (Spring 1989): 42.

69 Ibid, 44.

70 Ben Passarelli reminds us that around the turn of the century, the pioneer neurobiologist Santiago Ramon y Cajal had discovered that "the neural pathway for a reflex or recognition task cannot involve more than 20 or 30 sequential processing steps performed in parallel." In "Profiles in Learning," *Unix Review* 7:5 (Spring, 1989): 51.

71 Brody, "The Neural Computer," 45.

72 A. Wilson, "Do DARPA's Androids Dream of Electric Sheep?" *ESD The Electronic System Design Magazine* (July, 1988): 28.

73 Brody, "The Neural Computer," 47, 49.

74 Ibid., 49.

75 Wilson, "Electric Sheep," 30.

76 Passarelli, "Profiles in Learning," 52.

77 Maureen Caudill describes the difference: "A digital computer performs its actions on numbers that have been converted to a digital scale, of

course. This means that the numbers used can have only discrete values; they are not truly-continuous-values entries. The size of the discrete steps may be very small in practice (a 64-bit real number is extremely precise!), but the step sizes are there, in fact and the computer does not really handle continuous, analogue values," "Humanly Inspired," 42.

78 Herb Brody observes that the neural "network's function is determined by its topology—the way in which the neurons are interconnected . . . this also distinguishes neural networks from conventional computers, which rely primarily on a coded set of instructions, or program." "The Neural Computer," 44.

79 Ibid.

80 The most popular of these training procedures is called "back-propagation" and is described here by Maureen Caudill: "Back propagation networks use a training regimen called supervised learning in which an input pattern is fed into the network along with the appropriate output pattern for that input. Network interconnections weights are modified by the neurodes on the basis of differences between the network's actual output and the desired output. This process is repeated until the network correctly interprets the input patterns used for training. Thus, the training procedure is an interactive one, requiring many presentations of each training pattern before the learning is complete," "Humanly Inspired," 42.

81 John Naisbitt and Patricia Aburdene, *Megatrends 2000* (New York: Avon Books, 1990, 258).

82 Edward Hall, *The Silent Language* (Garden City, NY: Doubleday, 1959).

83 Kowinski, *The Malling of America*.

84 Quoted by Fred Thompson in "The Development of the Japanese Transportation System," *Explorations* 28 (Summer, 1970): 74.

85 Ibid., 76.

86 Ibid., 78.

87 Ibid., 84.

88 Mark Segal, "The Alien Other in Japanese Fantasy Television," *Canadian Journal of Political and Social Theory*, 12:3 (Fall, 1988).

89 Stephen Kline, "The Theatre of Consumption: On Comparing American and Japanese Advertising," *Candian Journal of Political and Social Theory*, 12: 3 (Fall, 1988): 104.

90 Ibid.

91 Nicholas Valéry, "Back to the Drawing Board: A Survey of Japanese Technology," *The Economist* (Dec. 2, 1989): 5.

92 Michel Random, *La stratégie de l'invisible* (Paris: Félin, 1985), 149–50 (author's translation).

93 Marshall McLuhan, *The Dew Line* (Toronto: McLuhan Centre for Technology, University of Toronto, Occasional Papers, n.d.).

94 Claudia Donà, "Invisible Design," in *Design after Modernism: Beyond the Object*, John Thackara (ed.) (London: Thames and Hudson, 1988).

95 Ibid.

96 McLuhan, ibid.

97 Ibid.

98 Pierre Lévy, *L'Intelligence collective* (Paris: La Découverte, 1994).

99 Jaron Lanier and Frank Biocca, "An Insider's View of the Future of Virtual Reality," *Journal of Communication* 42:4 (Autumn, 1992): 160.

100 Harold A. Innis, *The Bias of Communications* (Toronto: University of Toronto Press, 1951); *Empire and Communications* (Toronto: University of Toronto Press, 1972).

101 Havelock, *Preface to Plato*; "The Alphabetic Mind: A Gift of Greece to the Modern World, *Oral Tradition* 6 (1986): 134–50.

102 Havelock, "Prologue to Greek Literacy."

103 Marshall McLuhan, *The Gutenberg Galaxy: The Making of Typographic Man* (Toronto: University of Toronto Press, 1962); *Understanding Media* (Toronto: McGraw-Hill, 1964).

104 Elizabeth Eisenstein, *The Printing Press as a Agent of Change* (Cambridge: Cambridge University Press, 1979).

105 As David Harvey explains: " Symbolic orderings of space and time provide a framework for experience through which we learn who or what we are in society." Harvey goes on to quote French sociologist Pierre Bourdieu: "The reason why submission to the collective rhythms is so rigorously demanded is that the temporal forms or the spatial structures structure not only the group's representation of the world but the group itself, which orders itself in accordance with this representation." See David Harvey, *The Condition of Postmodernity: An Enquiry into the Origins of Cultural Change* (Cambridge: Blackwell, 1989), 214.

106 Schmandt-Besserat, "L'invention de l'écriture."

107 See Harvey, op. cit. 228: "Symbolized by clocks and bells that called workers to labour and merchants to market, separated from the 'natural' rhythms of agrarian life, and divorced from religious significations, merchants and masters created a new 'chronological net' in which daily life was caught."

108 Lanier and Biocca, "An Insider's View," 162.

109 McLuhan, *Understanding Media*.

110 Jean Baudrillard, *Les strategies fatales* (Paris: Gallimard, 1984).

111 McLuhan, notes from oral presentation, n.d.

112 Hans Kimmel, "The future of educational broadcasting," EBU *Review, Programmes, Adminstration, Law,* Vol XL, No. 5 (September 1989): 34

113 Peter Russell, *The Brain Book* (London: Routledge and Kegan Paul, 1979), 1.